The Mercy Seat

Thoughts Suggested by *The Lord's Prayer*

by
Gardiner Spring

author of
Distinguishing Traits of Christian Character
and *The Power of the Pulpit*

Edited by Dr. Don Kistler

Soli Deo Gloria Publications
. . . for instruction in righteousness . . .

Soli Deo Gloria Publications
P. O. Box 451, Morgan, PA 15064
(412) 221-1901/ FAX 221-1902
www.SDGbooks.com

*

The Mercy Seat was retypeset from the 1863 edition published in Glasgow. This Soli Deo Gloria reprint, in which spelling, grammar, and formatting changes have been made,

*

ISBN 1-57358-111-9

Contents

Our Father, which art in heaven,
Hallowed be Thy name.
Thy kingdom come.
Thy will be done,
In earth as it is in heaven.
Give us this day our daily bread.
And forgive us our debts
As we forgive our debtors.
And lead us not into temptation,
But deliver us from evil:
For Thine is the kingdom,
And the power,
And the glory forever.
Amen.

Chapter 1

General Observations on Prayer

The mercy seat was the covering of the ark of the covenant. At each end of this overshadowing oracle was a cherub of pure and massive gold, stretching out its wings, each towards the other, and forming a sort of throne. There was the visible emblem of the divine presence, and "God appeared in the cloud." There the high priest took the blood of the bullock of the sin offering, "and sprinkled it with his finger upon the mercy seat eastward, seven times." The book of the Law was there, protected by the ark of the covenant, and bearing the marks of atoning blood. It was God's throne of grace, and where the thrilling words were often addressed, "O Thou who art seated between the cherubim." It was the place of prayer: "There will I meet thee," said God to Moses, "and I will commune with thee from between the two cherubim which are upon the ark of the testimony."

I wish you, dear reader, to go with me to that mercy seat. I doubt not but that you have often been there, and listened to the instructions, as well as been comforted by the hopes uttered from the holy oracles. I am not introducing you to new scenes, nor do I profess to interest you with novel truths. There is nothing new on the subject of prayer. How can there be? It is addressed to the same Being by creatures of the same fallen character; it is expressive of the same affections, and under the influence of the same Spirit; it utters, for the most part, the same precious thoughts, and for the same ends.

There are men who have questioned the propriety of prayer, but they are those who, though they need the most, are slow to ask. There are those who feel insuperable objections to it, but they are only the objections of a prayerless heart. There are those who feel strong temptations to neglect it, but it is because Satan, that great deceiver, is well aware that the man whose home is the mercy seat is no longer the victim of his delusions. And there are those who have no comfort in it, and therefore restrain prayer before God. Yet there is no duty the Scriptures more explicitly enforce, no source of consolation which they more abundantly magnify.

Prayer is the language of desire; it is the offering up of our desires to God. It is the devotional thoughts and affections of the soul expressed in words. No spiritual emotions enter more intimately into the experience of the Christian, or more truly form the character of his piety, than those which are felt and expressed in his habitual intercourse with God. If he has adoring views of his Maker, and humbling views of himself; if he hungers and thirsts after righteousness; if he has strong confidence and joy; if his desires go out toward the enlargement and beautifying of the Church of God on the earth, and the salvation of men; nowhere do these internal emotions and desires find utterance so truly as in prayer. Where these devout affections exist with anything like ardour and intensity, they are uttered by a sort of necessity. Such persons cannot help praying. It is not possible that emotions this deep and spiritual, this high-born and heaven-imparted, should remain silent and smothered within the bosom. The heart is too deeply affected by them not to seek this relief.

Prayer is the language of nature because it is the language of desire and want. Even "the young lions, when they wander for lack of meat, cry unto God." The veriest infidel, the vilest atheist, in seasons of great public calamity, or personal danger and suffering, forget their infidelity and atheism, and pray. Emphatically, then, is it true of the Christian that he is a man of prayer. Though he knows that his neglect of prayer will not prevent the Father of mercies from causing His sun to shine upon the evil and the good, nor His rain from descending on the just and the unjust, his own heart will not allow him to live in that neglect. The divine bounty may still deck the earth with verdue and clothe it with fertility, and he may be a partaker of God's impartial goodness while it is unsolicited, yet there is something within his own heart that constrains him to pray. He has wants which nothing but prayer can supply; he has spiritual necessities, wants of the soul, which without prayer feeds on husks. Just as the plant strikes its roots into the ground to draw thence its vigor and nutriment; just as the flower opens its bosom to the sunlight and the dew, so the soul, by prayer, has communications with the God of all graces, and places itself under the kind influences of His love. It is like the stream cut off from its fountain, when it ceases to pray. It is like the plant that grows in the shade: pale and sickly, the sport of the winds, and blown about by the tempests of passion and the storms of the earth, because it does not seek this heavenly protection and nutriment.

Those who know most of the power of prayer are themselves the witnesses of the strength and fervor of its desires. None have felt more deeply than they that they cannot break the bondage of sin; nor, when once it is broken, can they enjoy the liberty of God's children without strong crying and many tears. Having escaped "the pollutions of the world through the knowledge of God their Savior," they are sure to be again "entangled in them and overcome" if they live without prayer. Those periods of their history in which their faith has been the most weak, their love cold, their zeal relaxed and wearied—when their relish for heavenly contemplation became dull and insipid, and they "savored not the things that be of God, but things that be of men," and when they cast their eye backward upon the world and its pleasures—were seasons in which their lukewarmness, if it did not shut them out of their closets, shut them out from all communion with God.

The degree of interest which men take in this religious service may be uniformly looked upon as a sort of moral barometer by which they may ascertain the elevations and depressions of their spiritual state. The mercy seat is the place where the Shekinah dwells, and where, beholding as in a glass the glory of the Lord, the suppliant is transformed into the same image, from glory to glory. It is the mountain top which catches the last rays of the sun when it no longer shines on the vale below.

The examples of prayer furnished in the Bible are exemplifications of true, sincere, and strong desire. The only rebukes to prayer ever uttered in the sacred volume are against those supplications in which the desires of the soul have no part, where the heart is wanting, and where the most solemn offerings are but "vain oblations."

Every gracious affection has both its aliment and expression in prayer. Its adoring love is there uttered, sometimes breaking out in the ecstacy of joy, and exclaiming, "Whom have I in heaven but Thee, and there is none on earth that I desire beside Thee!" There too are its expressions of penitence, weeping at the feet of mercy, sorrowing for the past, covering its face, and in prostration of soul before the offended Majesty of heaven, uttering its purposes of new obedience. There are the actings of its confidence, the simplicity of its trust in God, as well as the frequent renewal of that endearing and joyful submission to the divine claims which was the turning point in the sinner's progress from darkness to light. There too are the more abundant utterances of his gratitude. A thankful acknowledgment of God's mercies forms no small part of prayer. No man has received so few mercies that he has nothing to thank his Maker for when he approaches His throne in acts of worship. A sinner has reason for songs of praise as long as he is out of hell. Not returning thanks to God is one great reason why our prayers are not more frequently answered. Christians sometimes pray as if they had nothing to do but mourn. Ministers sometimes appear before God as the mouth of His Church, as if she was in a state of condemnation. This is unwarranted, and characterizes a spirit of bondage. "Be careful for nothing," says the apostle, "but in everything, by prayer and supplication, *with thanksgiving,* let your requests be made known unto God."

I would not want to offend God's children, much less would I want to depreciate the sighs of a broken, contrite heart, when I say that grief and mourning are not the only emotions which become the mercy seat. There is no fear of our ever being too penitent and humble. "The sacrifices of God are a broken spirit; a broken and contrite heart He will not despise." The prayer of the publican, when he stood afar off and smote upon his breast, saying, "God, be merciful to me, a sinner!" is a strong rebuke to the spirit of self-righteousness and Pharisaic self-complacency in prayer. There are seasons when the heart is so burdened with a sense of sin that it can do little else than mourn. But while these things are true, and are important truths, we are not to forget that "the fruit of the Spirit is love, peace, and joy." There may be self-righteous tears as well as hopes of self-righteousness. It is not unfitting in a sinner to call upon God "with joyful lips." The meek and subdued cheerfulness, the holy joy of piety, greatly honor the God of our salvation. If I am not mistaken, those are the most acceptable offerings, and those the most profitable seasons of prayer, and the most invigorationg for duty and trial, when the soul most rejoices in God through our Lord Jesus Christ.

Prayer is a humble, but not a servile spirit. There is more cheerful thanksgiving in the heart of a praying man than in all the men of the world put together. "I will bless the Lord," said the Psalmist, "at all times. His praise shall be continually in my mouth. My soul shall make her boast in the Lord; the humble shall hear thereof and be glad. O magnify the Lord with me, and let us exalt His name together."

Prayer is a very different thing from *saying* a prayer. As the language of desire, it is marked by great tenderness, great sincerity, and great simplicity. God, who searches the heart, has said that He does not acknowledge the worship of the lips. One great reason why the divine presence is so little felt in our devotional exercises is that our hearts are not in our prayers. Prayer brings the soul of man into contact with his Maker. How unlike that cold, formal, listless manner in which both those who pray and those who concur in this service often draw night to the mercy seat and practice their mockeries before God, even in His sanctuary.

The object of prayer is the living God. Nor let this be deemed too commonplace a thought; would that it had a place more common in the mind of every worshipper! There is no truth the Scriptures teach more frequently than that God is the *only* object of religious worship. To no mere creature on earth or in heaven may men bend the knee in prayer. "Thou shalt have no other gods before me." It is written, "Thou shalt worship the Lord thy God, and Him only shalt thou serve." The Bible knows nothing of the idolatries of that anti-Christian system of worship which justifies the use of images, and prayers offered to saints and angels. Notwithstanding the frivolous distinctions insisted on by the advocates of this system, as to the different kinds and degrees of religious homage thus paid to creatures, the minds of the great mass of the people are unaffected by these refinements. The practical influence of such worship is a positive encroachment on the honors of the supreme Being, who is a jealous God and will not give His glory to another. It is difficult to see how any mind, however constituted, can preserve the simplicity of its devotion and dependence unimpaired amidst these external symbols and multiplied objects of adoration.

Such is not the worship of the only living and true God. Of all this bowing at the shrines of departed saints; this reverence of the consecrated wafer; this adoration of the host; these votive offerings, and fervent, solemn invocations addressed to the Virgin; this entire machinery of the crucifix; the statues, the paintings, and all the apparatus by which theatrical effect is produced; and the imagination and senses captivated and enslaved—we may well say, "What meaneth this device?" The voice of God demands of all such idolaters, "Who hath required this at your hands?" Prayer is an act of worship. "Hearken unto the voice of my cry, my King and my God; for unto Thee will I pray." God alone is omnipresent to see the worshippers, and to hear their worship. "The eyes of the Lord are upon the righteous, and His ear is open to their cry." Only He can accept and answer their prayers. "The Lord is nigh unto all them that call upon Him, that call upon Him in truth. He will fulfill the desire of them that fear Him. He will also hear their cry, and will save them."

But if God is the only object of prayer, what is the way of access to Him? Is it through men? Or through the ministration of angels? Or by martyred saints? Or by our own merit and righteousness? These inquiries suggest solemn and affecting thoughts.

The character of the suppliants is sufficiently humbling; the Being they address, ineffably great and exalted. It is a most wonderful fact that abject man, man who is "fallen by his iniquity," should have intercourse with the high and holy One. On the lips of a sinning creature, that fearful name, the Lord thy God, is a name of solemn import. Oh, weigh the vast meaning of these words!

Well may a holy fear take possession of the heart, and awe it into reverence as it approaches the King eternal, immortal, and invisible. His greatness knows no bounds; His perfections are infinite; His spirituality is unmingled and pure; His existence has no beginning and will have no end. He is all-seeing, yet unseen; the most distant, yet the most near; comprehending all, and comprehended by none; containing all, while nothing contains Him. There is nothing but He controls it by His power; nothing but what lives and moves within the compass of His immensity. When spotless cherubim worship Him, they cover their faces with their wings, and "say one to another, 'Holy, holy, holy is the Lord God of hosts, the whole earth is full of His glory!' The wicked shall not stand in His sight, He hateth all the workers of iniquity." The nearer the sinful and polluted come to Him, the nearer they come to "a consuming fire." To the perverse, rebellious, and guilty children of the apostate race, His throne might well be overshadowed with clouds and darkness, and made repulsive and inaccessible. The glory of man is fallen; he is sunk in the dust; he has no wings to soar to the high privilege of communing with a holy God.

Yet even fallen man aspires after this; his desires, corrupted as they are, have a sort of inbred tendency towards something above and beyond this narrow world. He is not satisfied without God; nor can he ever be happy until he returns to the bosom of his aggrieved and forsaken Father. And, wondrous fact, men thus polluted and vile, instead of cringing as slaves before His throne under the terrifying expressions of His omnipotent justice, are drawn to it as sons by the attractions of His love.

There is "a new and living way into the holiest of all by the blood of Jesus Christ." Access to God as the hearer of prayer is the effect only of that great work of redeeming mercy in which the second Person of the ever-blessed and adorable Trinity came to seek and save those who were lost, and advance them to the privileges of children. We have nothing of our own to plead; yet in His name may our prayers go up as incense, and the lifting up of our hands as an acceptable sacrifice. Humbling and prostrating as the consideration is, we have not a rag of righteousness left us in which we may appear before the throne. The worthiness is not in us, but Christ's name, Christ's sacrifice, Christ's righteousness, Christ's work, and Christ's entire mediation as the atoning, interceding High Priest form the center and channel of all God's communications with apostate men, and the medium of their access to God. "For through Him we have access by one Spirit unto the Father." It is not possible for a sinner to find any other way of access.

In the religion of a sinner, the mediation of the Son of God is the great elementary principle. Natural religion is of no use to him, and only leads to the neglect of that which is revealed. Natural religion is only for beings who are sinless. As sinners, we can have nothing to do with God except through Christ. We have freedom of access only in that way which He has consecrated by His blood. We have no other. "I," said He, "am the way, and the truth, and the life; no man cometh unto the Father but by Me." He is the altar whence the hallowed incense arises, which is expressive of the purity and ardor of a true devotion. We have "an altar," says the apostle, "whereof they have no right to eat which serve at the tabernacle," an altar that abolishes all other altars, and is above every name. "The altar sanctifies the gift." And well it may sanctify it. It was erected not by the hands of men; the invisible God erected it on holy ground, in the center of this perishing world. There, "without the gate" of the Holy City, where God laid on Him the iniquity of us all, and the fires of eternal justice consumed the priest, the altar, and the sacrifice, that way to the mercy seat was opened, without which all amicable intercourse between heaven and earth had been forever suspended.

We dwell on the thought that prayer is offered in the name of Christ because, obvious as it is, it is both in theory and in practice a very important thought. Men have no more access to God than the devils have, save in this "new way which He hath consecrated through the veil, that is to say, His flesh." It is no small matter for a man, whose conscience is burdened by a sense of guilt, to find access. He who has never experienced this embarrassment has yet to learn that he is a sinner. We may be almost certain that if our prayers are put up in the name of Christ, and not answered, there is something wrong with them; and we may be quite certain there is everything wrong with them if they are not offered in the name of Christ. The promise is absolute: "Whatsoever ye shall ask the Father in My name, He will give it you." Yet to pray in the name of Christ is not simply to use the words. There is no spiritual spell in the mere words. They cannot charm away guilt, nor charm answers to our supplications. To pray in the name of Christ comprises a heart-felt acknowledgment of Him as the only appointed and accepted way to the throne. The mere intellectual perception of this truth is not enough. It must be believed and felt, with all its humbling, encouraging import; it must be received into the heart. The soul must have an immediate and direct reference to it in all her prayers; it must be confided in, and carried into the chamber of audience.

Prayer has power and influence. The spirit of prayer and the blessing of God have ever stood abreast, and gone hand in hand in His government of the world. "For all these things I will be inquired of by the house of Israel," says He, "to do it for them." A prayerless man is an unblessed man; a prayerless church is languid, inert, and unblessed. Those portions of God's heritage which have been most distinguished for the spirit of prayer have known most of the power and presence of God, and been most distinguished for the effusions of His Spirit. Whenever He is about to do great things for His people, He rouses them from their lukewarmness, and stirs them up to prayer.

There is no surer criterion by which to judge if God is about to do great things for them than an unusual spirit of prayer. It was so in the days of the Old Testament dispensation, and it is so under the New. It was so on the day of Pentecost, and it will be so when the scattered families of that same people are gathered in. "I will pour out upon them," says God, "the spirit of grace and supplication, and they shall look on Him whom they have pierced, and mourn." He "hath not said to the seed of Jacob, 'Seek ye My face,' in vain." "O Thou that hearest prayer" is one of the usual appellations by which He is addressed in Scripture. This is one of the names by which He is known, and this is His memorial to all generations.

No small part of the Scriptural history is employed in recounting the achievements of prayer. A selection of the prayers recorded in the Scriptures, with a detailed account of the manner in which they were answered, would form an instructive and edifying volume to the people of God. He has pledged His faithfulness as the hearer of prayer, to both His Son and to His people; and facts there recorded show, and facts hereafter to be recorded will show also, that He is not a man that He should lie, nor the son of man that He should repent. There is perhaps no more impressive proof of the power of prayer than the fact that God represents Himself as effected by the prayers of His people when He is about to make bare His arm in judgment against His enemies. "Let Me alone," said He to Moses, "that I may destroy this people." "I do not say that he shall pray for it," is a limitation confined to the unpardonable sin. It is indeed a marvelous truth, which God Himself has revealed, that "the effectual, fervent prayer of a righteous man availeth much." The men of prayer look for answers to their supplications, and they are warranted in so doing. One of the differences between the prayers of Christians and the prayers of other men is that the latter pray without minding the answers, while the former wait for an answer; and in substance, if not in form, and in God's own time, they get it.

Prayer, therefore, is an unspeakable privilege. For a creature, like fallen man, to be allowed to draw nigh to the Holy God, and express all the desires of his heart, in the name, and plead the full merits, of Him in whom the Eternal Father is well-pleased, is indeed the privilege of sons. Abject man, man who has fallen by his iniquity, enjoys this privilege. The hour of prayer is the appointed hour of this communion. Here the Father of mercies meets His offending creature with the smile of reconciliation; and here the creature, with a heart sprinkled from an evil conscience, meets his offended, but graciously reconciled, Father. There are few declarations in the Bible which, in the entire range of their instructions, are more richly fraught with the consolation which a sinner needs than the declaration made by God to Moses when He said, "And thou shalt make the mercy seat above upon the ark; and in the ark shalt put the testimony that I shall give thee. And there will I meet thee, and I will commune with thee from above the mercy seat." It is the communion of the created with the uncreated mind; a creature of yesterday holding converse with Him who is from everlasting; a creature who knows nothing in intimate and unembarrassed intercourse with Him who knows all things; one who for his abjectness is as a worm, and who for his sinfulness might make sackcloth his covering, tranquil and comforted in the presence of that holy Lord God.

Nor is there any longer any one appointed place of prayer. "In all places where I record My name," says He, "I will come unto thee, and I will bless thee." Territorial divisions, secular and ecclesiastical demarcations, and earthly distinctions, are all banished here. It is God's communion with the king and the beggar, with those who are near on the land, and those who are afar off upon the sea. True piety is the same thing every where, because God is every where the same object of worship, and the same hearer of prayer. To different climes, and all the different classes of men, to men of the various habits of thought, to men of manual toil and men of intellectual study, to the cool and tranquil philosopher, the patient historian, and the imaginative and ardent poet, the throne of grace brings substantially the same consolations, and calls forth the same warm emotions of grateful and adoring love, melting penitence, and implicit faith.

The duty of prayer is itself a delightful duty. It ordinarily presents the most lovely assemblage of those spiritual graces, and those intellectual perceptions and moral qualities of soul, in which true religion has been universally found to exist. There is no sweeter assemblage of gracious affections ever presented to that all-seeing eye which looks on the heart, and of which the renewed nature of man is conscious. And for this reason it presents the most lovely and most enviable assemblage of spiritual joys. If there is true blessedness anywhere, it is in the indulgence of such affections. They give pleasure to the mind; they are happy feelings so long as they exist, and afford the purest, the highest satisfaction of which sinful man is capable. There is additional joy, too, in the discovery of them; for though all may not be alike conscious of them, nor the same persons equally conscious at all times, there is a discovery of them at the throne of grace which is ordinarily made only there.

If there are good men who do not always enjoy the delightful conviction of their own gracious state in prayer, there are none who do not sometimes there enjoy it. No man should depreciate it because he cannot come so near the throne as Abraham came, or because he cannot converse with God face to face as Moses did; or because he cannot, like John, lean on the bosom of his Divine Lord, or because he may not, like Paul, be caught up into the third heavens. It is proof of the reality of his faith if he may there but lament its weakness. And if it is delightful to feel gracious affections at the throne of heaven's mercy; if it is delightful to be conscious of them; still more delightful is it to express them. It would be bondage and misery to express them unfelt; but to feel and express them, to be conscious of them and offer them to God, to make the offering in the name and on the merits of the Great Atoning High Priest, poor and humble as the offering is, it is itself adapted to gratify and invigorate these affections themselves, to increase and accumulate them. It is thus they become the consecrated conductors of spiritual blessings from God's high throne to many an otherwise depressed and mourning spirit on this low earth.

Secrets may be committed to God that cannot be committed to another. The world knows not of this relief, to spread before Him the secret wants of the soul; to tell them one by one; to tell them all. The conscience, wounded by a sense of sin, finds healing there. Want there finds supply; distrust finds confidence and depression finds praise. Ignorance is enlightened there; poverty is enriched, and weakness becomes strong. Darkness is there dissipated and trembling hopes encouraged.

The bruised reed is not broken there, nor is the smoking flax quenched. Grace there cherishes what it bestows, and completes what it begins. Spiritual enemies are there disarmed, or, if not disarmed, the armor is there for renewed and successful conflict. Angels' visits are few and far between, but the promises there habitually visit and refresh the soul, cheer its gloom, and comfort it when it is weary.

There are no broken cisterns at the mercy seat; it is all a fountain of living water, where streams flow from it, without which this earth were a desert. They who are most engaged in the duty of prayer have tasted most of its consolations. In the hour of trouble especially, it brings the soul near the only source of comfort. That man is truly wretched who, when earthly enjoyments fail, has no other to which he can resort; while he who can come to the footstool of God's mercy is never wretched. It is no barren land, but one where the heavens are opened, waters are poured upon him who is thirsty, and floods upon the dry ground. It is no place of storms and tempest, but a hiding from the storm, and from the tempest a safe covering. The region is pure because it is elevated; it is quiet and serene where faith, soaring in its flight, looks down upon earth and upward towards heaven. It is the sanctuary of God and where angels dwell. It is the rest of the soul. Ten thousand times ten thousand tongues, approaching it, have given utterance to the thought, "Return to thy rest, O my soul, for the Lord hath dealt bountifully with thee!" Like the disciples on the Mount of Transfiguration, they have often exclaimed, "Lord, it is good to be here!"

If the reader is living in the neglect of prayer, he knows neither his loss nor his danger. Many a man whose bosom is not a stranger to hope in God's mercy, can say, "But for this one privilege, I should long ago have perished, and gone down to the sides of the pit!" Men do not know the power of the sin that dwells in them who neglect to pray. Be admonished, O ye thoughtless ones, who "restrain prayer before God!" Their rock is not as our Rock; even our enemies themselves being judges. Men may have resources that are out of God, but they lean upon the same broken reeds which have pierced others through with many sorrows. Every thing else will deceive you; they are "lying vanities, and cannot profit." They are snares, and accomplish nothing more certainly than to entice the soul away from God, and deceive it to its undoing.

Be admonished, also, you who are careless and remiss in the exercise of prayer. However dissatisfied you may be with yourselves in this exercise, and however little you may have of the gift of prayer, "be faithful in that which is least." However little comfort you have in it, without it you will be left to a far more melancholy abandonment. Though your prayers may seem not to be answered, it is no proof that they are not answered because it is not in the time and way you prescribe. The old enemy tempts you when you little think that he is tempting you; and God is teaching you, when you yourself are not always conscious of His teaching. Prayer is the proper business of a man who is a sinner. He will never know how to live, nor how to die, if he is not a man of prayer. God gives liberally; He gives without upbraiding. He is as free to give the best gifts as the meanest, and to the most needy as much as to the least needy. He has no pardon for the sinless, no wisdom for the wise, no courage for the resolute, no strength for the strong, no hope for the presumptuous. "To this man," says He, "will I look, even to him that is of a poor and contrite spirit, and that trembleth at My Word." "This poor man cried, and the Lord heard, and saved him out of all his troubles." "When the poor and needy seek water, and there is none, and their tongue faileth for thirst, I the Lord will hear them. I the God of Israel will not forsake them."

Chapter 2

The Instructions of the Bible as to the Matter and Manner of Prayer

The incident is an interesting, and even a most beautiful one, which led the disciples of Christ to request Him to teach them to pray. He Himself had been praying; there was a simplicity, a propriety, a comprehensiveness, a fervor and spirituality in His prayer, that so instructed and affected them that they desired to sit at His feet, if it were but to learn how to pray. "And it came to pass, that as He was praying in a certain place, when He ceased, one of His disciples said unto Him, 'Lord, teach us to pray, as John also taught his disciples.' " Every Christian has an interest in knowing how the Savior would pray. The best of men need direction in prayer. Who may not adopt the language: "Teach us what we shall say unto Him, for we cannot order our speech by reason of darkness"?

How then shall we be instructed in the matter and manner of prayer? How shall an ignorant and guilty creature learn to address himself to the great Creator, who is God over all, blessed forever? The Bible is a sufficient rule of conduct in all things pertaining to life and godliness. The subject matter for prayer is to be found in the Word of God. There is not one of its doctrines, in all their richness and variety, that does not contain truths which the lips of prayer may make use of, and turn to good account at the throne of grace. What God is, what He has done, and what He has purposed and is disposed to do; what we are and what we need, are not less guides in prayer than they are principles of truth. "He that cometh to God must believe that He is, and that He is the rewarder of them that diligently seek Him." His love to the world in giving His Son to die, the condescension of His Son in laying down His life as a sacrifice for sin, and the work of the Holy Spirit in applying the truths of the Gospel to the soul, furnish not only the appropriate, but the indispensable aliment to the Spirit of supplication. "How shall they call on Him in whom they have not believed?" The point is too plain to require either illustration or proof: the mind must be furnished with the truth of God in order to be furnished with matter for prayer. Nor need we say more painful conviction of this than the absolute sterility and barrenness of thought, and worse than chilling coldness of those prayers, which it may have been our unhappiness to listen to, from men who deny the essential truths of Christianity. Socrates or Seneca, dwelling on the barren truths of natural religion, would have offered a richer prayer to the "unknown God" than I have heard from the hesitating and embarrassed lips of an unchristian ministry.

The precepts of the Bible also teach us how to pray. They describe the spirit of prayer; and they teach us what graces to ask for, and for what duties we need strength.

The promises of the Bible are revealed for our instruction and encouragement in prayer. They teach us what blessings God is willing to bestow, and how willing He is to bestow them. They are "exceedingly great and precious"; they are wonderfully various, adapted to all cases of want, and all the varieties of Christian experience. They are promises for health, strength, food, and raiment; they are promises of peace, safety, success, courage, and comfort. They are adapted to seasons of temptation, sickness, poverty, persecution, calumny, darkness, and fear. They are promises of light, of regeneration, of repentance, of faith, of peace, of joy, and of the indwelling witness of the Holy Spirit. They are promises of obedience, of perseverance in holiness, of the coming of God's kingdom on the earth, of calmness and hope in death, and of eternal glory. Nor is there one of them that does not give a fresh impulse to the soul who wrestles at the throne, and that may not be used as an argument in prayer.

The threatenings of the Bible teach us what we have reason to fear and deprecate, while the very sins that are there recorded teach what we should pray against and deplore. "All these things," says the apostle, "happened unto them for examples; and they were written for our admonition, upon whom the ends of the world are come."

God has also recorded a multitude of facts in His Word that are comments upon its truths, its promises, and its threatenings, of which He condescends to permit His people to remind Him, and which furnish them with powerful considerations in pleading at His mercy seat. They are facts which belong to the history of His dealings with good and bad men, with nations and individuals, with the Church and the world.

There are instances of prayer, too, there recorded, which show us its spirit, its comprehensiveness, its appropriateness to times, and places, and circumstances, and men, as well as its fruit and power; and which show us for what it is to be offered, and God's readiness to hear and answer. The Bible tells of Moses, Elias, Daniel, and Job, who set their face to seek the Lord God by prayer and supplication. God has there recorded also a great variety of the experiences of His people, and of His own conduct towards them, and of their supplications under the dealings of His hand. Of all the books in the Bible, the book of Psalms is the one which is fitted to teach men how to pray, and how they do pray when influenced by His Spirit. In this book, the Spirit of God has delineated His own operations on the hearts of His people. The book, generally, is nothing more nor less than a diagram of a good man's heart, the inside section of a believer's soul.

More than this, the Bible teaches us where to go for assistance in prayer. "For through Him we have access by one Spirit unto the Father." In every act of true devotion, there is a concurrence of the Spirit's influence. No man is wise enough or holy enough, or sufficiently acquainted with his own wants, or with the mind and will of God, to pray as he ought to pray, unless directed and assisted by the Spirit of God. With the most guileless sincerity, apostles themselves acknowledge, "For we know not what we should pray for as we ought; but the Spirit itself maketh intercession for us with groanings that cannot be uttered. And He that searcheth the heart, knoweth the mind of the Spirit, because He maketh intercession for the saints according to the will of God." Men are ignorant, forgetful, and erring; but the Spirit "helpeth their infirmities" by enlightening their understandings, assisting their memories, warming their hearts, and directing their desires in prayer after right objects. It is no marvel that men who pray, without feeling their dependence on God's Spirit and seeking His aid, offer disconnected prayers, random prayers, and prayers that have no object. Prayers they may be that are fluent, but they mean nothing; they are wordy prayers, destitute of thought and emotion, because those who offer them have forgotten that they are not sufficient of themselves to think anything of themselves. It is the work of the Spirit to teach men to pray. The heart and the tongue must be under His influence. "Open Thou my lips, and my mouth shall show forth Thy praise." The prayer that reaches heaven must come from heaven.

It is the Comforter alone who imparts the spirit of adoption, whereby we say, "Abba, Father." "The preparation of the heart in man, and the answer of the tongue, is of the Lord." The Spirit of God Himself is called "the Spirit of supplication." It is He who prays in the people of God; and when He teaches them to pray, it is "with all prayer and supplication in the Spirit."

On every page of the Bible there is matter for prayer, and he who would pray with intelligence and fervor must study his Bible. The best instruction we can give on this subject is to refer you to the Bible. Let the Spirit of God impress you with a sense of your wants and direct your desires. Let your mind be richly furnished with all God's truth, and let your bosom be filled with devotional emotions, and then freely utter your requests before God. There is thought in prayer, strong thought, and often close, compact, and connected thought. There is emotion, too, heavenly emotion. There is memory in prayer; and there is conscience and even imagination. There is the argument of Moses, the piety of Isaiah and David in prayer; and the fittest combination of them all, directed by God's Spirit, uttered with simplicity and fervor, and with no burdensome restrictions upon the heart, constitutes the sweetest, humblest, most grateful and heavenly devotion. To aim at eloquence in prayer is, of all abominations, one of the greatest; to affect singularity in it is the strangest of all affectations. There is a copiousness of diction in the prayers of some Christians which is not found in others; and there is an unusual copiousness in the same Christian at different seasons and under the power of different thoughts and emotions. All this is natural, for "there is a diversity of gifts, but the same Spirit."

But this is not all the instruction the Bible gives in relation to the matter and manner of prayer. While it contains the principles by which we are to apply the matter of prayer, there is a special rule of direction in what is commonly called "the Lord's Prayer." I cannot help thinking it is a mistake to call it so, because it is a prayer which our Lord Himself could not use;

it contains confessions of sin which He could not make. If there is a prayer in the Bible which may be properly called "the Lord's Prayer," it is contained in John 17, a prayer which no other than He could ever offer. This formula contains the substance of prayer for His disciples. In no other part of the Bible is the service of prayer so methodically specified. It reduces the matter of prayer to certain great subjects, under one or other of which all lawful requests may be presented. It is distinguished for great tenderness, great sincerity, great simplicity and precision, giving us the different headingss of prayer, and at the same time giving us the whole range of the Bible for matter to put under these headings.

A question arises here whether we may use this form in our supplications at the throne of grace. Most certainly we may; most certainly we do; most certainly we ought, though there is no evidence that we ought to do so uniformly and always. The Christian ought not to be so much the enemy of forms as to depreciate this most beautiful form of prayer; nor so much of a formalist as not to pray without it. That we must use it as a form not to depart from, as if there was some charm in the words, is not conceded.

We are naturally led in our inquiries on the general subject of prayer to a consideration of the question of praying with or without a prescribed form. There has been, and is still, a great variance in the belief and practice of professed Christians in the manner of addressing the throne of grace in this particular. Some churches have set and stereotyped forms, prescribed by ecclesiastical authority, even upon their archbishops, their bishops, their presbyters, and their deacons. It has never before fallen in this writer's way to speak extensively upon this subject; nor does he do it now without some misgivings—misgivings not of truth and principle, but misgivings arising form the fact that, as a general axiom, it is no part of true religion to find fault with the religion of other people.

I would preface what I am about to say with this single remark: in this matter, "Let every man be fully persuaded in his own mind." If there are those who, from conscientious convictions of duty, give an honest preference to forms of religious worship, they may well say to us, who honestly differ from them, "Who art thou that judgest another man's servant? To his own Master he standeth or falleth." Since, however, our own principles and practice are dear to us, we hope it will not be deemed unfitting or uncharitable to advert to some of the considerations by which they may be defended. This we shall do without embarrassment, though without designing to give offence to those who differ from us, unless they are offended by God's truth.

Jesus Christ has nowhere authorized a restriction to any set form of prayer. The only passage in the New Testament which has the semblance of this authority is the declaration made by Him in relation to what is called "the Lord's Prayer": "After this manner pray ye." My position here is that the Savior gave His disciples this prayer not as a form in words, but in substance and manner. He does not say "after these words"; His object was to furnish His disciples hints on the subject of prayer; nor could they, from the nature of the case, be entitled to expect any thing more. The most rigid advocates of forms do not profess to believe that by the instructions here given the Savior designed to limit His Church to these words, or even to these thoughts; because they themselves have with great care and pains presented other and more amplified forms. To us it seems that a fair mind must confess that the Great Teacher here designed to furnish His people with the great outlines of prayer, without attempting to draw out the whole system of devotion, and filling up all the parts of it. Men of prayer will readily class these several topics, and naturally remember and resort to them when they pray. There is not one of them that is extraneous and foreign to the subject of prayer, nor any one of them which, when prayer is offered upon a large scale, may be omitted. The order is natural, and the transition from one thought to another is such that it is not abruptly made; nor is the mind at all embarrassed in perceiving the association of thought which connects the whole. It covers the common wants of man; so far as it goes, it is adapted to all the stages of Christian experience, and no less fitted to the babe in Christ than to those of mature age.

The sacred Scriptures nowhere speak of reading prayers, nor make any allusion to a liturgy. Would they not have done this if established forms of prayer were indispensable to the prosperity of the Church, or the comfort and beauty of her worship? The prayers of Abraham were not written prayers. Nor was the prayer of Eleazar at Haran, nor the prayer of Jacob at Peniel, nor the prayers of Moses and Aaron for Egypt and Israel. The prayer of Joshua at the defeat of Ai, the prayer of Manoah, of Samson, of Hannah, of Samuel at Mizpeh, of Elijah at Mount Carmel, of Hezekiah against Sennacherib, of Jabez, of Ezra, of Nehemiah, of Job, of Daniel, of Jonah, and of Habakkuk, were none of them dictated by the pen. Nor was the prayer of Zacharias, nor that of the publican, nor that of the disciples in any one exigence of their history. The prayers offered by the disciples of Christ subsequent to the period when He thus taught them, that are recorded at length in the Acts of the Apostles, grew out of the peculiar condition in which they were offered, and were offered under the impulse of their peculiar exigences; yet in not one of them is there one word of the Lord's Prayer, nor even the remotest allusion to it. The prayer of the apostles upon the appointment of Matthias to the apostleship, their prayer on the release of Peter and John from the Jewish Council, and Paul's noble supplication, recorded in Ephesians 3, have not the slightest reference to the Lord's Prayer, but in method and thought are entirely different from it throughout. They were prayers for special occasions, called for by the occasion itself, offered without the least restriction by this prescribed form, and under circumstances in which this form of prayer would have been altogether inappropriate. There are also instructions on the subject of prayer scattered throughout the epistles, in addition to those given in the Lord's Prayer, and which this form does not include. We are taught to offer all our supplications in the name of Christ, which this prayer says nothing about; this evidently teaches us that there are other and superadded revelations on this subject, and that this form, excellent as it is, is not the sole directory. Jesus Christ, therefore, has nowhere authorized a restriction to any set form of prayer.

In the next place, forms of prayer invert the order of prayer; they make the words lead the heart, and not the heart the words. True prayer flows from the heart, the seat of supplication. This truth is, indeed, so obvious that the best writers, who are the strenuous advocates of forms, contend for them only as aids to the worship of the heart. But in doing this they do no more, even by their own showing, than make the lips affect the heart—whereas the nature of the case, the meaning of the terms, and the uniform teachings of God's Word, make the heart in prayer affect the lips. It is in prayer as it is in speaking: before a man speaks he must have something to say; his thoughts must first give an impulse to his tongue. Before he prays he must have thoughts and emotions to utter; his heart must move first, his lips afterwards. This is the true order of prayer. God first gives the heart to pray, and then the words. He does not give the words first and afterwards the heart. In every instance—in the beginning, during the progress, and at the close of prayer—the heart goes before the lips, and not the lips before the heart.

A man's mind and affections may be excited by the sound of his own voice in prayer, and one sentence of supplication may thus prepare the way for another; but the incitement is produced by the utterance of thoughts and emotions already existing within his own mind. They are not vain words which move him, but thought acting upon thought, emotion upon emotion, each and every one of them taking precedence of the utterance of his lips. No man begins prayer with mere words, as forms teach him to do. We do not deny but the heart may follow the words; we only affirm that the words ought to follow the heart. When we read in the Scriptures of men stirring themselves up to take hold on God, who does not see that this is an intellectual and spiritual stirring up, and not a rhetorical effort? It is not an effort of the lips to affect the heart, but an effort of the heart to affect the lips. And hence it is that an habitual reliance upon forms of prayer encourages spiritual sloth and an idle mind, and tempts men who read or repeat a prayer to be careless of self-examination, and too little solicitous of exciting grace in the heart to pray. We do not say men are hypocrites whose religious worship is restricted by forms; on the other hand, we have no doubt of the piety of many of them; while of the piety of not a few, we have evidence of the most convincing and delightful kind. But we say that the natural tendency of their system is to encourage hypocrisy. There may be hypocrites who pray without a form; but they are more exposed to be hypocrites who are induced to believe that saying the prescribed words of prayer is prayer.

With regard to secret prayer, the true and natural idea of it is that it is a man's own mind and heart that prays, while the one who uses the prayers that are made for him by another makes use of the mind and heart of another, and not his own. There is danger of hypocrisy, and still more of honest self-deception, everywhere; but the danger is greatly increased where the words professedly lead the heart, and not the heart the words. I do not judge other men—I know not the influence of habit on their own minds—but to me it appears a very strange thing that a Christian man, much more a Christian minister, should wish to find his prayers written in a book.

Another objection to forms is that they check the teachings of the Holy Spirit. If what has been said in relation to the work of the Holy Spirit in prayer in a previous paragraph is true, I do not know how to get over this difficulty; it is absolutely fatal to the whole system of forms of prayer, save in those cases where they are necessarily imposed as leading-strings in childhood and ignorance. God has promised to give the Spirit of prayer and supplication. For what? To indite our own petitions at His throne. Does the man need this influence who finds them already indited in a book? It may be said that he needs this influence to enable him to enter into the import of the prescribed form, but it is nowhere promised for this purpose. He has no certain evidence that the original authors of the form he uses were influenced by the Spirit of God; for while God has promised to give the Spirit of prayer to those who pray, He has nowhere promised to give His Spirit to any man, or any set of men, to enable them to write prayers for other people.

And what is still more to our purpose, the Apostle Paul, in giving an account of the work of the Spirit on the Christian's heart in prayer, says, "Likewise the Spirit also helpeth our infirmities, for we know not what we should pray for as we ought." Now, if we use prayers that are made for us, it is not true that we do not know what we should pray for as we ought. We do know, because we have all our requests before us in the book. Either we do know or we do not. If we do not, then in using forms our own requests are not offered. If we do, the apostle is sadly mistaken. But the mistake is not Paul's; it is in the book of prayer, which professes to know what we should pray for as we ought, which the Spirit of God says we do not know, and which He Himself teaches us when we ourselves pray.

Retired, and sometimes sweet and awful, are the secrets between the soul of man and God. "What man knoweth the things of a man, save the spirit of a man which is in him?" And who searches and develops them in prayer but the Spirit of God, whose influence forms of prayer supersede, and who Himself alone searches the deep things of God?

Still another objection to forms of prayer is that no set of prayers is, or ever can be, adequate to the necessities of the Church. Who does not see that, however excellent any liturgy may be, and however great the variety of its forms, it is a simple impossibility, without the aid of a new revelation, and without the spirit of prophecy, to form a set of prayers that shall suit a Church at any period of time hereafter? Hence we find that new editions of the Book of Common Prayer are continually making their appearance. By common consent and authority it has been altered, abridged, enlarged, amended, and otherwise disposed of according to the various exigences of times and occasions. The Church of England has, in the reign of several princes, since the first compiling of her liturgy in the time of Edward VI, not only made unessential alterations, but alterations in the main body and essential parts of it. And she must do so again if she would cut off the complaints of her own members.

Yet with all this liberty, no form can meet their exigences. When events take place in the providences of God, for which the prescribed forms of prayer furnish no appropriate and adequate supply, the whole Church must stand still and wait until the constituted authorities prepare a new form of prayer, and publicly authorize the use of it. No one, not even her ministers or bishops, may go beyond the prayer written in his book, however unexpected, extraordinary, and urgent the demand may be for some marked and strong peculiarity in their devotions.

If, from public and social prayer, we go to the devotions of the family and the closet, the embarrassment is increased a thousandfold. Every family, and every individual, has mercies of their own to be thankful for, sins of their own to confess, and wants to be presented before God, which no prescribed form can reach; and to be limited by such a form is an encroachment upon Christian liberty and privilege to which no heart or conscience ought to be subjected. The primitive Christians and churches knew nothing of such a restriction, nor would they have submitted to such bondage, not for an hour. Hence no small part of the devotions of the papal and episcopal churches consists of vain repetitions, of disjointed prayers, of shreds and fragments of prayer, which have no connection with each other, and which are far from presenting anything like a continuous address to the throne of grace.

We may add that forms of prayers are, in their nature, absurd and preposterous. The spirit of prayer never requires men to pray in any set form of words. Its emotions are so various that it must necessarily seek its own way of expressing them; they are often full, and such as cannot be suppressed, but must give themselves utterance in a way adapted to their own strength and tenderness. A hungry beggar does not ask alms, nor a drowning man cry for relief, only by a set form. The idea would be preposterous. No more does a perishing sinner plead for mercy and grace to help in the time of need by a set form. The great controversy between God and His visible people in every age has arisen from the strong tendency of the human heart to satisfy itself with mere forms. It relates to a spiritual religion on the one hand and a formal religion on the other. From the corrupt state of the Church in the days of the prophet Isaiah, down to the Pharisaic formality, which was so severely rebuked by the Savior, and from that time to the present, this is the great subject matter of controversy. Is it not safe to be on the right side of this great question?

Such are my objection to forms of prayer. Let me not, however, do the injustice to advert exclusively to the considerations against them, but give all due weight to the considerations which have been suggested in their favor.

It has been said that the example of the primitive Christians is in favor of forms. Much has been written to prove the antiquity of liturgies, and Bishop Bull has strongly urged the probability of their being of apostolic origin. The Church of England has preserved in her *Book of Common Prayer* some prayers of ancient date, to which she attaches great importance from their mere antiquity. But were the example of Christians, even from the days of the apostles to the present hour, in favor of forms, so long as there is no warrant for them in the Word of God, it lays no obligation on our consciences.

The statement itself, however, that the example of the primitive Christians is in favor of forms, is not true. The posture of the primitive Christians in prayer was such as to render it impossible to read prayers. They stood with their arms crossed on their breasts, their heads back, and their eyes often closed. It is confidently asserted by those who have made close search that there is not such an expression as "reading prayers" to be found in the history of the first four centuries. The most eminent ritualist the Church of England has produced for a hundred years confesses that the public services of the primitive Church were all performed *extempore,* or *memoriter,* and that no one office was reduced to writing until the fourth century.

After this, we know there were set forms of prayer, but it was an age of remarkable degeneracy and corruption; and it was super-induced and came on by a punctilious and superstitious regard for modes and forms of worship. There is no fact better established than that, for several centuries after the resurrection of Christ, prescribed forms of prayer were unknown. When strict inquisition was made for the books of the Christians by their persecutors, it was a singular fact that their Bibles were demanded, and not a word is said of their prayer books. So when the Emperor Constantine, in his zeal for Christianity, directed the Christians to be supplied with the Bible, he said not a word about prayer books. In early ages, too, very many of the clergy, and not one of the common people, could read; and what good could prayer books do? The Christian families of that illiterate age must either have worshipped God without forms of prayer, or not worshipped Him at all. We have also the expressed testimony of the early Christian fathers on this subject. When Justin Martyr is describing the worship of the second century, he said that the officiating minister offers up prayer and thanksgiving, according to his ability, an expression which would be unmeaning if he had read prayers from a book. Tertullian too, in the same century, says, "We pray without a monitor, because we pray from the heart."

In favor of forms, it is also said that it is important to have matter to ponder upon in order to pray with intelligence. I have only to reply that most certainly it is so; but then there is more matter in the Bible than in a *Book of Common Prayer*.

It is further urged, and we confess the objection has some weight, that in extemporaneous prayers too much latitude is given to the speaker, so much so that, on the one hand, his prayers may often be barren and dry, and, on the other, they may be redundant, and sometimes filled even with wild and extravagant notions. This is true; it is an evil to be guarded against; and I have only to say that we expect too much when we expect perfect prayers from imperfect men. And are there no such imperfections in the reading of forms of prayer? Are they never recited with chilling coldness and schoolboy negligence? In order to remedy these evils, I have heard them chanted!

But what would the Savior and His apostles have thought of setting their prayers to music? Besides, are there no imperfections in the forms themselves? Is the extravagant praise so gratuitously bestowed upon the liturgy of the Episcopal Church the praise that is due to it? Does it insist upon no arrogant pretensions? Does it inculcate no superstitious rites? Does it teach no errors in doctrine? Has it no defects and no redundancies? "I have no hesitation in saying," says the late Dr. [Thomas] Dick of Glasgow, "that in other churches prayers far superior are offered up every Sabbath; and I have frequently heard a prayer poured out by a man of God, with the assistance of the Holy Ghost, which, in my judgment, was more valuable than the whole of the liturgy."

Carry out the principle of the objection, and it militates equally against the whole Gospel dispensation. A minister has the same liberty in preparing his sermons as in uttering his prayers. On the principle of the objection, we must have a set of sermons prepared as well as prayers. And the Church of England has, in former days, acted upon this principle, and prepared her Books of Homilies, or discourses for her ministers. But they were days of ignorance which God winked at, and which the Church winked at because the clergy were not then qualified for their office. She discontinues this latter usage because she has, to a very considerable extent, an intelligent and devout clergy; and the reason is equally applicable for discontinuing her prescribed form of words in prayer.

It is objected to prayers that are not thus formed that the

people cannot join in them. I might here reply, let the experience of the Christian world who have never embarrassed themselves with forms answer this objection. Is it so that there is among us no such thing as joining in prayer? The objection assumes what is not true in fact. It assumes also what is not true in the philosophy of the human mind, and that is that its operations are slow. Men as easily follow the suppliant in prayers as they do the preacher in his preaching. So rapid are the movements of the mind that in a praying assembly there are hundreds of digressions from the prayer that is put up by the speaker, without the loss of a single thought that he utters. The petitions of the speaker are made the petitions of the hearers, while every man of prayer among them is secretly putting up his own requests, all the while suggested by the thoughts of the speaker, and all of them ascending as sweet incense to the throne through the great High Priest of their profession to His Father and their Father, to His God and their God.

I say no more; perhaps I have already said too much. Beware of a state of heart in which you feel the want of a book to teach you to pray. It may be advisable in cases of need to use a form at the family altar; better pray with a form than not pray at all. Yet never use a form unless, after patient effort and long seeking the Spirit of God to teach you to pray, you find that you cannot do without it. Trust no council, bishop, or pope to make your prayers for you. Look at all the Bible and learn how to pray. Pray as you want. Feel your wants, and then let your heart utter them without embarrassment. When God says, "Seek ye My face," let your heart reply, "Thy face, O Lord, will I seek." Alas, that there should be a prayerless heart in such a world as this, where the God of heaven has erected His mercy seat, and where He dwells on purpose to hear the supplications of sinful men!

Chapter 3

God Is A Father
"Our Father, which art in heaven."

It is said to have been a remark of the late Madame De Stael that the prayer of which this is the first sentence was itself sufficient proof of the truth of Christianity. No fair mind can deny that the prayer itself is a remarkable production. The amount of truth it embodies, its high morality, and deep, touching devotion, are such that no mere philosopher or sage could have been its author.

"Have we not all one Father?" said the prophet. "Hath not one God created us?" If the minutest atom does not exist without the first great Cause, that wondrous and complex being, man, could never have been the production of chance or accident. If the form and features cannot be even transformed to the painted canvas without the skill of the cunning artist, much less is the living original the production of a blind fatuity. "Fearfully and wonderfully made" is the high distinction stamped on the man the creature. The eye, the ear, the tongue, the hand, nay, every organ, muscle, and nerve of his material frame, all indicate an intelligent and designing Creator. That single organ, the heart, repeating with such wondrous regularity its equable pulsations some sixty times every minute for three score years and ten, has no equal within the whole compass of mechanical invention; nor is it in the power of language to express a greater absurdity than that it does not indicate the hand and agency of a wise and almighty designer. The meanest of the race, too, is invested with an intellectual, moral, and accountable nature; the flame of undying thought is lit up within him, and wondrous susceptibilities have a dwelling in his warm bosom. The great and almighty Parent breathed into the cold clay the breath of life, "and man became a living soul."

It has often been questioned if a speculative atheist ever existed. It is a remark of Cicero that "there never was a man who constantly and absolutely denied a god." Pure atheism, or the absolute denial of an intelligent first cause, is rarely to be met with; but that there have been, and still are, modifications of atheism may hardly be denied. Gross thoughtlessness, eager inspection of the apparent inequalities in the divine government, extreme depravity of manners, the enormous absurdity of vulgar superstitions, the affection of singularity, and the desire of seeming wiser than others, skepticism on other moral subjects, and the refinements of false science, as well as the weak and inconclusive arguments which have sometimes been employed to prove the being of a God have, there is reason to fear, shaken the faith of men in this fundamental truth of all natural religion. But whatever the forms or the causes of this radical error, it has no apology in the reason, or even the prepossessions of the human mind. "I had rather believe," says Lord Bacon, "all the fables in the Legend, the Talmud, and the Koran, than that this universal frame is without a mind." As the Psalmist tells us, it is the fool who has said in his heart, "There is no God."

A strong and practical belief in the divine being and presence lies at the base of all true devotion. An atheist cannot pray, for "He that cometh to God must believe that He is, and that He is a rewarder of them that diligently seek Him." Men sometimes utter the words of prayer without seriously thinking of Him to whom they pray; and though they believe there is a God, they pray as if there were none. They do not deny His being, they merely disregard it. They are "without God in the world." "God is not in all their thoughts." For all they love, fear, or hope for, God might as well not exist. Such prayer is an abomination. Prayer is the language of nature because it is the language of want; it is the language of a creature to his Creator; of a child, dependent, helpless, and benighted, to his unearthly Parent. The pagan poet, referred to by Paul in his appeal to the philosophers of Greece, made no unnatural avowal when he said, "For we are also His offspring." Without distinction of age, character, condition, or faith, the enlightened and the ignorant, Jews, Mohammedans, Pagans, and Christians, those who dwell on the land and those who are afar off upon the sea, may all look upward, and say, "Our Father, who art in heaven!" There is not one of them who is not the object of His paternal care and bounty, whom He does not instruct with a father's counsel, restrain and govern with a father's authority, and whom His hand has not been stretched forth ten thousand times to keep from falling into destruction. From whatever station in human life, portion of the world, or degraded state of human society; from whatever throne or dungeon; from whatever liberty or servitude any one of the vast family of man may affectionately and dutifully address his thoughts to heaven, he shall find a father's ear, and the heart of a father. His family is large and widely dispersed; it is composed of millions upon millions, scattered over every continent and island, every sea and shore, every mountain and valley, every palace and every log cabin; nor is any one of them denied the relation of children. They are His property: He made them for Himself, and He owns and cares for them.

One of the obligations of piety is founded on this natural relation which men sustain to God as the parent source of their being. There is indeed a higher claim; but we need look for none that is more imperative in order to originate our obligations to filial love and obedience. "If I be a Father," says He, "where is Mine honor? If I be a Master, where is My fear?" What rights of sovereignty are comprised in this single relation! The potter has power over the clay, of the same lump to make one vessel unto honor and another unto dishonor, yet the clay is not the potter's creature. Men in authority say to one, "Go," and he goes, and to their servants, "Do this," and they do it; yet these are but conventional claims, and have no such deep and immutable foundation as those which result from the relation of man to his Maker. These are bonds which, however violated, cannot be dissolved, but must remain in full force and obligation as long as God and creatures exist, and are what they are. Time cannot alter them; no condition of suffering or of joy can alter them; they remain unaltered to all eternity. Men will not pray unless they acknowledge them; nor is it any unusual thing for them to "cast off fear and restrain prayer," because this very service of prayer itself strengthens and confirms their obligations to Him in whom they live, move, and have their being. There is value in this relation. Men feel it in the hour of danger and distress, even though at heart they know not God. They look to Him and are enlightened. His tender mercies are over all His works. It is not a matter of indifference to Him whether they live or die. He who hears the young lions when they wander for lack of meat hears the cry of distress. It is not in His heart of tenderness and love to turn a deaf ear to the sighs of human misery, come they from whose bosom they may. He, who commended His love toward us in that when we were enemies Christ died for us, and who when we were dead in sin quickened us, with all His just hatred of their character, has a heart of pity. When agitated by fear, and depressed by despondency, from the ends of the earth even may such sinners cry unto Him. There is no promise in the Bible which entitles them to a hearing, while there is the tenderness of the divine compassion, that rebukes their despair and urges them to penitence.

I have said that there are higher claims than these. When we adopt the language, "Our Father, who art in heaven," we are also reminded of the still more endearing relation which exists between the Heavenly Father and those who constitute His spiritual family. God has a family of His own on the earth, a "peculiar people" in distinction from the rest of mankind. To the earlier invitations to incorporate themselves with this spiritual family, men turned a deaf ear; they made light of them, and all began to make excuses. It is only when they fall in with these gracious overtures that men become the children of God. They are more than creatures; they are affectionate and dutiful children. They are no more strangers and foreigners, but fellow-citizens with the saints, and of the household of God. From the far wandering where they perish with hunger, they come home to their heavenly Father's house, where there is bread enough and to spare. This is a high and holy relationship. To be God's creature merely does not constitute it. Birth in a Christian land does not constitute it. Descent from a pious ancestry does not constitute it. Holy baptism does not constitute it; nor is it constituted by any mere outward forms, professions, or services. Many a man sustains an outward and visible relation to God's family, enjoys all the immunities which such relation furnishes, and passes under the external bond of God's covenant, to whom none of these things give a passport to His kingdom, and who is in the end an outcast.

The Scriptures and facts instruct us that every son and daughter of Adam is by nature alienated from God and a child of wrath. He is destitute of holiness, unpardoned, unblessed, and has no natural rights except for the just reward of his iniquity and the inheritance of the fallen. When we speak of a child by adoption, we do not mean a child by nature. We speak of adopting a stranger, an orphan, or an outcast; and this is the adoption to which we refer when we would indicate the spiritual family of God. It is the free, gracious adoption of an unworthy, guilty, and condemned, but now reconciled and pardoned sinner. "That which is born of the flesh is flesh, and that which is born of the Spirit is spirit." There is a first birth, and there is a second, one that is spiritual and from above. It is this new birth which is the starting point in the spiritual career, and which draws the dividing line between those who are aliens and those who are children. Born of earth only, they have the image of the earthly; it is not until they are "born not of blood, nor of the will of the flesh, nor of the will of man, but of God," that they bear the image of the heavenly. It is no more the law of nature that children resemble their parents than it is the law of grace that the children of God resemble their heavenly Father. It is by no natural agencies, and no common method, that men thus become God's children. "Ye are the children of God," said the apostle, "by faith in Jesus Christ." He is the honored One in this gracious arrangement. "God sent forth His Son, born of a woman, made under the law, to redeem them that were under the law, that we might receive the adoption of sons." The great object of His advent and sacrifice was to take out from the mass of men a people to His praise; to separate from this ruined race a family, redeemed by His blood, sanctified by His Spirit, and bearing the resemblance and name of their Father who is in heaven. He thus descended that they might ascend. He became an obscure child of one of the families of earth so that they, through Him, and through faith in His name, might become allied to the families of heaven. Though He was the Son of God, He became the Son of Man, so that they, though the sons of men, might become the children of God.

There is a great difference between the creature of God coming to God as His Creator, and with no other encouragement than the flickering hopes that are warranted by the lights of reason and nature, and coming to God in the new and living way opened up by Jesus Christ. There is a great difference between the sinner under condemnation coming to the Judge of all, and the Christian thus coming to His heavenly Father.

Even under the old dispensation, the people of God were not denied the hopes and consolations of this filial relation. The language of Moses to the people of Israel was, "Ye are the children of the Lord your God." "Doubtless Thou art our Father" was the language of the prophet. "Though Abraham be ignorant of us, and Israel acknowledge us not, Thou art our Father, our Redeemer; Thy name is from everlasting." In the same strain of pensive confidence he goes on to say, "But now, O Lord, Thou art our Father; behold, see we beseech Thee, we are all Thy people!" And again, in the words of another prophet, it is written, "Wilt thou not from this time cry unto Me, 'My Father, Thou art the guide of my youth?' "

But this is not the ordinary language of that less illumined age. Under the old dispensation, the Holy Spirit in believers was, to no small extent, the spirit of bondage; under the new, it is that of adoption. The privilege of calling God their Father was not so fully known because "the new and living way into the holiest of all was not yet made manifest." Those ancient saints had beheld fearful exhibitions of the Deity; to them He was "fearful" even "in His praises." He had said that He would "dwell in the thick darkness." The Christian's view, in approaching the throne of grace, is that God is his Father. "Abba, Father!" is his cry. However great his unworthiness and ill-desert, it is his privilege to come as a child, an heir of God, and a fellow-heir with Christ His Son. The truth cannot be too frequently inculcated that there is but one way of access unto God in any of His institutions. Every other way is but some modification of Deism.

The punishment of sin is necessary because of sin. When a sinner approaches God with the confidence of a child, he honors the great propitiation made by His coequal Son. The eternal Father is well pleased to have this effective mediation thus put to the test by all who call upon Him. He would have us address Him by this new name, "Our Father," a name so entwined with the dearest associations of the human heart. And it is in delightful keeping with His nature, who will not break the bruised reed, and will not quench the smoking flax, to teach His disciples thus to pray. Never was sight more interesting and lovely on earth than this; and many a miniature of it, though faint indeed, I doubt not is engraven on the memory of millions. Who first taught us to pray, as Christ taught His disciples? Who can forget the time or the place when he buried his face in his mother's bosom, or knelt at her feet, and repeated the words from her lips, "Our Father, who art in heaven"?

The eccentric but remarkable John Randolph was once heard to say that he would probably have been an atheist but for his tender remembrance of his devout mother making him kneel by her side and, taking his little hands in hers, teaching him to say, "Our Father, who art in heaven." Would not many of us have been atheists had we not, in the gracious providence of God, thus been taught to pray? Our Father! blessed relation! Thrice-blessed Savior, thus to instruct the guilty children of men! That He should appropriate such language as this is not strange, but that He should instruct us to appropriate it may well lead us to exclaim, "Behold, what manner of love is this, that we should be called the sons of God!"

The beautiful language of this prayer is, "Our Father." There are two thoughts of interest in this emphatic phraseology. "Thou art my God," said the Psalmist, "and I will exalt Thee." Elsewhere he says, "God, our own God, shall bless us." There are the actings of an appropriating faith in words like these. When the Savior showed Thomas His wounded hands and feet, he exclaimed, "My Lord and my God!" Faith is a humble grace, a self-renouncing grace, but it is a trusting confidence. God is in Christ, reconciling the world to Himself; when the believer receives Him, he receives Him for his own soul. He is his own God. It is a privilege to call Him "Father," but a greater privilege to be enabled by His Spirit to say, in the language of this prayer, "Our Father."

We would no longer lie
Like slaves beneath the throne;
Our faith shall Abba, Father! cry,
And thou the kindred own.

Whatever is expressed by that comprehensive word, the faith of the suppliant receives as his own and for his own benefit. God's fatherly love is his; His power and faithfulness is his; all the perfections of the Godhead are his, pledged for his security and ultimate salvation. Such is the privilege of faith, and of all the children of God. No unbeliever can thus use the words of this prayer. Every such man is a stranger to this filial relation because there is not a trace of filial affection towards God within his cold, suspicious, and hostile bosom. He has not the adoption of sons; and they are sons only who can thus say, "Our Father."

But this is not all which these cheering words express. The social character of this prayer may not be passed over in silence. It is "Our Father." The social character of religion is too little known by the men of the world, and appreciated too little by Christians. It is an egregious error, into which many have fallen who know nothing of Christianity but its name, that it is a morose and cheerless thing; that it is made up of useless sacrifices and joyless self denial; and that, instead of being welcomed to the very bosom of human society, its proper place is the solitary mountain, the lonely chamber, the sequestered grove, or the cold monastery. True piety has indeed much to do with individual character and obligations. It cannot exist without secret meditation and solitary communion with God. It becomes rank and poisonous without the retirement of self-inspection and secret prayer. It withers and dies without those hallowed feelings and affections that are unseen by mortal eye, and those unuttered breathings of the soul that are unheard by mortal ears. Yet is it designed to call into exercise and consecrate all the social principles of our nature.

There are common interests, and there are individual interests, to be prosecuted in joint supplication. God is not only the hearer of prayer, but the hearer of social prayer. There can be no family wisely constituted that is without it. Wherever God records His name, there will He meet His people and bless them socially. No two individuals can be connected together who have not some common interest as the ground of joint supplication. The same may be said of larger bodies of men. Every legislature that is convened for enacting laws and the purposes of government should unitedly and daily seek the guidance and blessing of heaven. Every ship that floats on the ocean should be vocal with prayer.

But especially is this the social privilege of the Church of God. All her prayers are founded on the principle that, as an associated community, she is composed of God's children, and approaches His throne as accepted in the Beloved. Those who oppose social prayer do not love prayer at all. Social prayers, for things that belong to the social relations, are heard and answered. It is as much the constitution of God's moral government that bodies of men, who have a common interest, offer prayers for common wants as it is the constitution of His providence that individuals offer them for individual wants. The Author of this prayer was divine, yet a man like ourselves; and because He was no stranger to our sympathies, He has left the reviving promise: "Where two or three are met together in My name, there am I in the midst of them." The primitive Christians were eminently spiritual, but their religion was strongly marked by its social character. It consisted in their "walking together in all the commandments and ordinances of the Lord blamelessly" in refreshing one another in their languor and fatigue, cheering one another in their depression, inspiriting one another in their thorny and often sanguinary way.

Why should it not always be thus? Is it that there are any necessary elements of dissension in the society of Christians, or that those who love God, and whom God loves, have not the strongest inducements to love one another? Men who have accepted the offers of the divine mercy, as sinners, who have been renewed by the Divine Spirit, and reconciled to God by faith in His Son; who are the purchase of His blood, the subjects of His kingdom, the children of His family, and the heirs of His glory, strangely forget the bond that constitutes them as one society when they do not love as brethren. That sublime address, "Our Father, which art in heaven," is an everlasting rebuke to all such Christians. Numbers unite in this act of worship. All have virtually united in it for eighteen centuries; and all will unite in it to the end of time. "Our Father" binds all Christians in one. It leaps every external barrier, surmounts the obstacles of birth and station, wealth and talent, and disregards the shades and colors of denomination and difference; nay, it overlooks infirmities and faults, and asks only, before it gives the right hand of fellowship to the partaker of its own apostasy and hopes, "Is he a Christian? Does he love Jesus Christ? Does he believe in the Son of God? Does he do the will of his Father who is in heaven?"

The social relations flourish only under the genial influence of Christianity. They have never been known in their purity in pagan lands, however elevated by science, and refined by the courtesies of life. Those sentiments of predilection, those principles of elective affinity, and those laws of association which govern men and bodies of men, who are themselves ungoverned by the gospel, are for the most part false and treacherous, impure in their origin, sinful in their nature and designs, and melancholy in their consequences. The gospel alone purifies and elevates them, and gives them principle. "Our Father which art in heaven!" How strong the bond! Here the worst affections are subdued, and the best called into exercise. Here every principle of truth and goodness is confirmed, every devotional feeling strengthened, and piety becomes invested with new attractions. The powers of earth and sin are here subdued—suspicion and jealousy, envy and hatred. Here the motives to mutual forbearance and confidence acquire increased force; and common hopes, hopes full of immortality, become the foretaste and earnest of holier and happier associations in a more holy and happy world.

Nor may the thought be lost sight of that union is the soul and strength of prayer. If united action is powerful action, so united prayer is powerful prayer. That one phrase, "Our Father," is a voice from heaven calling upon all the children of God to cultivate more assiduously the spirit, and practice more faithfully the duty, of united prayer. "If two of you shall agree on earth as touching anything they shall ask, it shall be done for them of My Father who is in heaven." Why should the social principle be pressed into every other service save the service of God? And why, while men associate for the purposes of business, pleasure, literature, accomplishments, science, and the arts, are there so few associations for prayer? Shall every other society be sought rather than the society of God's children? Shall men be ambitious for fellowship with those who occupy a large place in this world's consideration, and shall they be ashamed of those who have no higher honors than that they are the disciples of Jesus? There is something unutterably delightful, sweetly subduing, and universally humanizing in the bond which thus has its origin far above this low earth, which survives the changes of this world, which receives solidity from its afflictions and sufferings, becomes the stronger from all that threatens it, is indissoluble to the ravages of death, and grows purer and brighter forever.

There is also in this brief address a sublime ascription. "Our Father, which art in heaven." The Divine Being is not confined either to the heavens or the earth. He "filleth all in all." There is no height so lofty and no depth so unfathomable, no place so unoccupied and no void so empty and extensive, that He does not occupy it. " 'Am I a God at hand, and not a God afar off,' saith the Lord? 'Do I not fill heaven and earth,' saith the Lord?" Neither land, nor sea, nor heaven, nor hell, nor light, nor darkness, contains the place where He does not dwell.

But though this great and universal Parent is everywhere, there is strong propriety in fixing our thoughts upon Him in prayer as a Being in every way exalted, and far above all creatures. We may not think of our Father who is in heaven as we think of any other being in the universe, nor address Him as we address another. He is in heaven, highly exalted as God over all, reigning there in invisible majesty, and dwelling in light that is inaccessible and full of glory. He is venerable for His greatness. He decks Himself with light as with a garment, and is arrayed in majesty and excellency. He stretches out the heavens as a pavilion. He lays the beams of His chambers in the waters. He makes the clouds His chariot, and walks upon the wings of the wind. The alterations of day and night, cold and heat, and all the varieties of the seasons, are determined by Him. He commands the sun and it rises not, and He seals up the stars. He makes Arcturus, Orion, Pleiades, and the chambers of the south. He does great things that are past finding out, yea, and wonders without number. He makes His angels spirits, His ministers a flaming fire. Clouds and darkness are round about Him; justice and judgment are the habitation of His throne. A fire goes before Him and burns up His enemies round about. His lightnings enlighten the world, and the earth sees and trembles. The hills melt like wax at the presence of the Lord, at the presence of the Lord of the whole earth. The heavens declare His righteousness, and all the people see His glory. We call Him our Father while angels bow before Him, and before the splendor of His glory cover their faces with their wings. With what sacred emotions ought such a Being to be approached! And how wondrous the condescension is that He should point us to His mercy seat and say, "There will I meet you, and there will I commune with you!" Oh, let us lift up our hands with our heart to this God who dwells in the heavens! Be not rash with your mouth, and let not your heart be hasty to utter anything before God; no thoughtlessness, no impertinence, no irreverent familiarity may be indulged with the great God. The nearer the soul approaches to Him, the more profound the reverence. There is reverence in the more familiar and confiding exercises and expressions of filial love. We reverence earthly parents, but He is our Father who is in heaven. Heaven is the place He has chosen for the seat of His glory, where the splendor of His divinity shines, whence He issues forth the decrees of His providence, and where He proclaims Himself, and the myriads who stand in His presence proclaim Him, the King eternal, immortal, and invisible.

Thoughts like these are searching thoughts. A child may deceive an earthly parent, but God cannot be deceived, and He will not be mocked. "All things are open and naked to the eye of Him with whom we have to do." Lost, indeed, would that child be to all virtuous and honorable feelings who, amid scenes of folly and wickedness, would not shrink from the inspection of a father's eye. We have a Father whose inspection of our every thought is minute and constant, who asks no informer to acquaint Him with our wickedness, no testimony to confound us before Him and clothe us with shame, if we come to His throne with disingenuousness and insincerity.

But they are also comforting thoughts. There is great imperfection in earthly parents compared with God. Earthly parents know not how to adapt their bounty at all times to the wants of their children. They give when they ought not to give, and withhold when they ought not to withhold. There is no such defect, and no such mistake with God. When earthly parents would fain give to their children, they are not able. The poor cannot give of their penury; and where competence, and wealth even, fall to the lot of parents, there are wants which no opulence can supply. But nothing restricts God's power to give: giving does not impoverish Him, and withholding does not enrich Him.

The love of earthly parents is strong; it survives separation, annihilates distance, and forgives disobedience, rebellion and neglect. It does not perish even with the infamy of its objects, nor will it yield its claims to the stern and inevitable demands of the grave. It outlives life, feeds on recollected joy and hopes, and lavishes on the marble and on the turf that tenderness of which the dead are unconscious. It is self-sacrificing and uncomplaining, coveting even weariness, watchings, and pain for those it loves. But it is not indestructible. Other objects sometimes supersede its claims. Coldness has extinguished it; desertion and neglect have quenched its glowing embers; it has often yielded to prejudice, and perished under the power of lust and superstition. "Can a woman forget her sucking child? Yea, they may forget," says our Father who is in heaven, "yet will I not forget thee!" Whom He loves, He loves to the end. Heaven and earth shall pass away, but this faithful word of love and mercy shall never pass away. Earthly parents die; they dwell in houses of clay; their foundation is in the dust, and they are crushed before the moth. The brow that bears the marks of care and toil becomes pale and cold; the hands that minister to the wants of those who are most beloved must be paralyzed in the grave; the tongue of wisdom must be silent in that narrow house where there is no work, nor wisdom, nor device; and the heart that beats for us must soon beat its last throb, and sleep beneath the clods of the valley.

It is not so with our Father who is in heaven. Around the grave of the fondest earthly parent, the children of God may exclaim, "The Lord liveth, and blessed be my Rock, and let the God of my salvation be exalted." Time passes, but does not shorten His duration. Years roll away upon years, while He still lives in the bloom of His eternity. The expressions of parental love cannot follow those on whom they are lavished to the grave, and protect them from corruption and the worm; nor can they go with them up to the bar of judgment, and shield them from the sentence of a violated law. It is a corruptible inheritance only which they can leave to their children, to be divided among them for a brief period in this transitory world. Their Father, who is in heaven, distributes to His children honors that are unwasting; an inheritance which is "incorruptible, undefiled, and that fadeth not away," a building of God, a house not made with hands, eternal in the heavens. In their Father's house are many mansions. Their home is above the clouds. God Himself is the heritage of His people, their heaven, and their exceeding great reward.

And they are also grateful thoughts. It has been objected regarding the Lord's Prayer that it contains no ascription of thanksgiving. But is there no feeling of tender love, of grateful, subduing remembrance, when from the heart we say, "Our Father, who art in heaven"? Is there no recognition of inexhaustible bounty, boundless beneficence, rivers of love, oceans of mercy, a generosity so disinterested and noble, and a tenderness so touching, that it would be impossible to give utterance to our deep sense of them in any language half so compendiously and forcibly as in these few words? This great and good Being, this King eternal, immortal, and invisible, writes His name, "Our Father," and this gives us access to Him as His children! The condescension is His, the privilege is ours. What have we to be thankful for compared with this? What has all the world to offer compared with the privilege of calling God our Father!

Let the spirit of this first sentence in the Lord's Prayer counsel us to cherish more befitting impressions of the God we worship. He is no unbending tyrant, no hard master, but the best and kindest of fathers. Vengeance is not the attribute He delights in; rather He delights in mercy. Oh, how little do they know of God who clothe Him only with terrors, and refuse to hope in His mercy? He is terrible only to incorrigible wickedness; to the penitent He is gentle and mild, like a nurse towards her children. Away with this jealousy and suspicion, this distrust, fear, and aversion, when contemplating the character of your Father who is in heaven. There is no sternness and repulsiveness in that Holy One, who teaches His children to call Him "Father." It is not with a frown of wrath upon His brow, nor with menaced damnation on His lips, nor with the thunderbolt of vengeance in His hand, that He invites sinners to His throne. There are other discoveries of the divine nature than these. There is the heart of love; there is the infinitude of love, since He is "not willing that any should perish, but that all should come to repentance." There is not one among all those to whom His gospel is known who does not have the warrant to accept these great provisions of their heavenly Father's love. Those who are afar off may draw nigh; those who are aliens and enemies may become children, and be adopted into His divine family. "Behold," said He, "I stand at the door and knock; if any man hears My voice, and opens the door, I will come in and sup with him, and he with Me." Though unworthy of the privilege, though we cannot acquire it by any works of righteousness, though the gold of Ophir cannot purchase it, it is a privilege that He gives. He gives as an affectionate father gives to his son, as a wealthy, bountiful prince adopts some poor orphan, and makes him the inheritor of his crown.

Come, then, you who are young! No longer despise the bounty and grace of your Father who is in heaven. Come and enter into His family, whose faithful love will guard you from the sins that embitter, and the woes that await all who are strangers to the living God. Now, while conscience is yet tender, and memory and heart are open to impressions that will leave their trace upon many a passing year; now, "while the evil days come not," remember your Creator in the days of your youth. He utters no stronger and no more affectionate claim than when He says, "My son, give Me thy heart." He would have those wayward and wandering thoughts, those dissipated, vain, and idolatrous affections, weaned from others and concentrated on Himself. Child of promise and of hope, of solicitude and prayer, thoughtless and gay, and never more in need of a father's care, will you not from this time say unto Him, "My Father! Thou art the Guide of my youth"?

You, too, who are absorbed in the earth, infatuated by its pleasures, burdened with its business, or grasping after its wealth and honors! Come and seek the repose, and set your affections on the inheritance which earth has not, and which pertains only to the family of God. "Wherefore spend ye your money for that which is not bread, and your labor for that which satisfieth not?" Powerless as this world is to make you happy, it is mighty to destroy you. Why, pilgrims and strangers on earth, do you give that to the world, the fashion of which passes away, the affections which are due only to Him who lives forever and ever? " 'Wherefore, come ye out from among them, and be ye separate,' saith the Lord, 'and touch not the unclean thing; and I will receive you, and will be a Father unto you, and ye shall be My sons and daughters,' saith the Lord Almighty."

You children of sorrow, to you the voice of mercy declares that the man is never comfortless who has God for his Father. Trials are no longer trials when the burden is cast on the bosom of His paternal love. Sorrow loses its name when His own soft hand wipes away the tear. Consolation in the woes of earth is not in forgetfulness, nor in gaiety, nor in braving the ills which are impossible to avoid. Miserable comforters are they all!

You whose earthly parents have descended to the tomb, and left you to prove the chilling negligence and selfishness of this cold world, how unutterably precious for you to learn the lesson: "When my father and mother forsake me, then the Lord will take me up!" Let not your heart be troubled, He will not leave you orphans. Think not that your last hope lies buried among the dead. Weep not in such bitter anguish at that grave. Do not say, "Oh, I wish I were resting with you beneath that tranquil clod!" Your Father who is in heaven shall never die. He has said, "I will never leave you, nor forsake you!"

You, too, who are disappointed and mortified in the world, who are sick of men because they have so often deceived you—come, make the eternal God your refuge. You whose hopes have leaned on earth only to learn that in one sad hour the bright vision may vanish, come and lean on an arm that is never weary, and partake of bounty that is never exhausted. You, too, who may perhaps complain of earthly parents, come and make the God of heaven your Father. There is one of whose care and tenderness you shall never complain, of whose liberality you shall indulge no suspicion, and who, while all the objects of love and expectation here below prove to be broken cisterns that hold no water, Himself remains the Fountain of living waters.

And you who have no God, oh, return to the God from whom you have revolted, the heavenly Parent you have so ungratefully forsaken, and who, by so many and such various means, would fain induce you, prodigal as you may be, to look towards your Father's house. What a void, what a chasm there is in that bosom that has no God, no Father! How true to nature is such a prayer! How dear to nature are the precious truths it reveals! Return, poor exile, to your forsaken Father. Come, you wanderer, you long-lost spirit; come back at your Father's bidding. Here is His letter to you, inviting you to come. Here is His name and seal. Are they not your Father's?

In the secret of your closet, then, return to Him. In the silence of your heart, return to Him. In mourning and penitence, in confidence in His Son, in peace and joy, come back to Him. And then, when you die to sin on earth, you will live unto God and heaven; you will go to your Father's house, and where He is, there shall you be also.

Chapter 4

The Name of God is to be Hallowed
"Hallowed be Thy Name"

This formula of prayer bears the same relation to the subject matter of prayer as the ten precepts of the Decalogue do to the whole subject of obedience. As the latter, under some one or other of its precepts, comprehends whatever is man's duty in any situation; so the former, under some one or other of its petitions, contains every request that a man need offer to the throne of grace. "Hallowed be Thy name" is the first of these comprehensive petitions.

The order in which the desires of a devout mind are here directed to be expressed, corresponds with the object of the Deity in creation, providence, and redemption. There is no truth more clearly revealed, or more consonant to reason, than that God should have the glory. Wherever we look around His works, they are marked with excellence; not with the excellence of the creature, but of the Creator, who is "God over all, blessed forevermore." When you compare all created excellence with His, it is as nothing. It is great to us, but we are small. Put all the excellence and all the enjoyment which appear in the manifestations of His goodness in the balance with Himself, and they are as the dust of the balance. That which is finite can bear no assignable proportion to that which is infinite. So that whether we stand on the basis of Scripture or sober reason, no end should be so steadily pursued as the glory of God.

Such would be the religion of nature had not man fallen by his iniquity. Such is the religion of the Bible, and of fallen man, redeemed man, and glorified man. There is but one object who is enthroned in the heart of piety, and that is the infinitely blessed and adorable God. Everything else occupies a place second and subordinate to His honor and glory. The first promptings of prayer, therefore, are uttered in the language of reverential piety towards God. Above ourselves, above all creatures, above all that is in earth or in heaven, we approach His throne to express our supreme regard for Him. And how do we express that regard? "Hallowed be Thy name" is the first desire of a believer's heart. Let us now analyze this great request.

"Name" is that which distinguishes a particular object, or person, from all others. This is universally its meaning, whether applied to classes of men or to individuals. When applied to God, it denotes all that distinguishes Him from anything that is created. Whatever is peculiar to the living God belongs to His name. Its most correct, simple, and comprehensive definition is "all that whereby He maketh Himself known."

He says of Himself, "I AM that I am; that is My name." He assumes the name JEHOVAH; this is properly the incommunicable name of God. The Jews had such a reverence for it that it was with them an unuttered name; and it is worthy of remark that there are no epithets associated with this name more than two or three times in the Scriptures. Every peculiar appellation which God assumes belongs to that name, because by that appellation He makes something known. If He speaks of Himself as "The Only Wise," He teaches us His perfect and unerring wisdom; if as Almighty, He teaches us that He acts without constraint, and that He can do all things. Whenever the distinctive name of Jehovah is given as the ground of confidence for some good being performed to the Church, it has reference to that proclamation made to Moses when He covered him by His hand in the rock of Horeb, and passed by and proclaimed His name in the fullness and amplitude of His wondrous and adorable attributes.

There was no appeal to God's name by the Church prior to this as ground of her confidence. It is in view of this proclamation that she exclaims, "Do not abhor us for Thy name's sake," and that David prays, "For Thy name's sake, O Jehovah, pardon mine iniquity, for it is great." There is a proportion between God's great pardon and His great name.

The name of God expresses great and wondrous thoughts. It is a name of solemn, awful, and yet blessed import. It points to the infinite, eternal, and unchangeable One. It points to the Father of mercies and the God of all grace. It points to our Father who is in heaven. Oh, weigh the vast meaning of His name, who is able to save and to destroy, whose favor is life and whose frown is death!

We pray that His name may be hallowed. To hallow is to sanctify; but as God cannot be sanctified or made more holy than He is, we must use the term with some restriction. To hallow God's name is to magnify, to honor, and to glorify it. It is written in the prophecy, "Sanctify the Lord of Hosts Himself, and let Him be your fear, and let Him be your dread." When we use the expression, it denotes our ascribing to Him all holiness, goodness, justice, mercy, and truth, forever enriching and adoring His great and glorious nature. It denotes our esteem of Him, our conviction that He is worthy of our confidence; and when we thus sanctify Him, He will not only be our fear and our dread, but our sanctuary in the day of trouble.

It denotes, too, the spirit with which we should worship Him. Its language is, "Give unto the Lord the glory due unto His name; bring an offering, and come into His courts. Oh, worship the Lord in the beauty of holiness; fear before Him, all the earth." The Scriptures often speak of the glory of God, and of glorifying His name. Here the Word is hallowed, because His holiness comprises the beauty and excellence of His nature, and constitutes the true glory of His attributes. The seraphim over the mercy seat covered their faces with their two wings, and cried one to another and said, "Holy, holy, holy, is the Lord of Hosts; the whole earth is full of His glory!"

In expressing this first and greatest desire of every devout mind, it is of some importance to institute the inquiry, "How is so desirable an end to be brought about? We confess our inability to honor God aright. We ask that He would make us fit to honor Him, and to give Him the glory which is due Him."

This is done, in the first place, by our becoming acquainted with God. Many a man fails of receiving due honor from his fellowmen because he is not known. We need but to become acquainted with His excellencies in order to love and respect Him. His excellencies may be unpresuming and retired, and need searching out; or they may be obscured by His humble condition or covered by a veil of prejudice, and require inspection by an impartial eye, that they may be appreciated. No man honors God while he remains ignorant of Him. Paul represents it as the crime of the heathen that "they did not like to retain God in their knowledge"; and so far were they from hallowing His name that they "worshipped and served the creature." It is the sin of all ungodly men that "there is none among them that understandeth, none that seeketh after God." Pharaoh, in his pride, said, "I know not the Lord, neither will I let Israel go." It was the Savior's reproach of the Jews that they did not know Him who sent Him. No other knowledge, however extensive and minute, will qualify us to respect and honor God, where the knowledge of God Himself is wanting. Let the most profound philosopher examine the whole circle of human knowledge; let him study every art and science; let him penetrate the bowels of the earth and the caverns of the ocean; let him number the stars and trace the revolution of the planets—and if he does not dive deeper, and does not ascend higher than this, the humble peasant whose devout study is to become acquainted with God better honors and hallows His great and holy name.

I mourn to confess that the religious worship of not a few is degrading to the Deity. On their very altars is found the inscription, "To the unknown God." The knowledge of God opens to the mind the only honor which He will accept, the only honor the creature is capable of expressing, and the only way of expressing that honor. We respect the Deity from a consideration of His divine excellence; nor can we fail, at least, to respect Him if we know Him. To dishonor Him when we know what He is would be impiety bordering on the foolhardiness of devils.

The name of God is also hallowed by a reverential treatment of Him in our thoughts, words, and actions. "As a man thinketh in his heart, so is he." Low, unworthy thoughts of God will lead neither to complacency, gratitude, nor honor. Whence is it that multitudes who once had low and unworthy thoughts of God now regard Him with solemn and affectionate reverence, but that they do justice to Him in their own reflections, and that, of all beings in the universe, He stands the first in their esteem?

With such thoughts of God, we must reverence Him with our lips. Our words must be words of deep reverence, sincere piety, and grateful love, whether we speak to Him or of Him. The careless and frequent mention of His name in our familiar intercourse with our fellow men; occasional exclamations, however heedless, which contain that great name, and which are the effect of sudden passion or surprise, as well as solemn appeals to Almighty God under no sense of His majesty and purity are plain violations of the true import of this prayer.

There is one way of dishonoring God of which I need say nothing except to bring it to your remembrance. I mean profane swearing. God will judge the swearer, and will not hold him guiltless. It is terrible to think of a man who learns to swear before he learns to pray. Cursing and blaspheming are the employment of devils. The profane swearer will have enough of it in hell. When the worm gnaws and the fire rages, he will curse God and look upward.

A reverential treatment of God in our thoughts and words will lead to the same treatment in our conduct. If we would venerate God, we should be watchful not to offend Him, nor dishonor Him by our deportment, nor bring His cause into contempt, and cause His name to be evil spoken of. A dutiful child will avoid those courses of conduct which bring reproach and dishonor upon his parents; so ought the children of God to be afraid of sin for His name's sake. God is honored when our deportment exhibits every mark of respect and honor. He is venerated when our conduct venerates Him, and His name is hallowed when our light so shines before men that others, seeing our good works, glorify our Father who is in heaven.

There is no lack of those who accost the Deity under the most respectful titles; they call Him "God," "Lord God," and "Great and glorious God," yet they disobey His laws, and mean to disobey them. The Savior animadverted upon this inconsistency when He demanded of such persons, "Why call ye Me 'Lord, Lord,' and do not the things which I say?" There is no greater inconsistency than to acknowledge His rightful authority, and at the same time practically disown His claims. To pray that His name be hallowed, yet not hallow it by our own obedience, is an indignity which reason, conscience, and decency instinctively revolt at. Men may be better in their own view, they may appear better in the sight of their fellow men, and they may think they appear better in the sight of God by an ostensible acknowledgment of His claims while they practically disavow them; but it is an expression of homage which God does not regard. Nor do men regard it once they discover its disgraceful inconsistency. The name of God is hallowed before the world only as His claims are practically honored, and their excellence exemplified. Unfriendly as the world is to these claims, it will no longer hiss and wag its head in derision and contempt of them when it sees them exhibited and acted out in the deportment of those who profess to regard them.

God's name is hallowed by a suitable regard to all His institutions and ordinances. The knowledge and worship of God are preserved in our world by a watchful and zealous regard for His own institutions. Under the Mosaic economy, these were greatly multiplied; under the Christian dispensation, they are less numerous and more simple. Men have added to them by their own traditions, but they are additions subversive of Christianity and of the simplicity that is in Christ. Christianity weeps over this perversion of her rites, and in the multitude and confusion of these outward ceremonies may well adopt the lamentation of Mary, when she said, "They have taken away my Lord, and I know not where they have laid Him." They are the mere outward defenses of "another gospel," from which the indwelling Spirit of Christ has retired, and His glory departed.

Just as truth is in order to goodness, institutions are for the sake of principles; and such are all the institutions of a pure Christianity. The institutions which the Great Founder of religion has appointed coincide with the great end for which the entire system of Christianity itself was revealed. They are the visible symbols of great and important principles, and the means by which they are advanced and perpetuated. The gospel cannot live without them. Prostrate these, and you exterminate true religion from the earth. They are the bulwarks which its enemies never fail to attack, in order to bring it into neglect and contempt. Men who would honor the name of God, and render it a hallowed name, will have a care neither to neglect, pervert, or corrupt these sacred institutions. The more punctually and constantly they are observed, the more are they rendered amiable and honorable in the eyes of the world, and the more they give honor to that Great Being who is their Author. When the soul is elevated with a view of His grandeur, rapt in the contemplations of His glory, melted under impressions of His love, and gives utterance to its admiration, its gratitude, its contrition, its hope, its confidence, and joy in those varied acts of worship which the institutions of the gospel require, she sympathizes with the homage paid to Him by higher worlds, and adds her testimony to theirs that His name is above every name.

The name of God is also hallowed by the exhibitions which He Himself makes of His own excellence. It is impossible to add to the immeasurable plentitude of God. It is not for creatures to make Him greater or better than He is; nor can God Himself do this because His essential perfections are every way infinite.

But though the perfection of the divine nature admits of no accessions, there may be accessions to those manifestations of the divine nature which are made in the works of providence and grace. There is an intrinsic excellence of the Deity which admits of no augmentation; and there is a manifested excellence which admits of augmentations that are boundless. From the richness and fullness of the divine character, there may issue streams, emanations, a diffusion and resplendency which may refresh and enlighten the world, and make the name of God great and glorious in the eyes of angels and men.

When we pray that God's name may be hallowed, we pray that He Himself would make it holy and venerable by more and more extended and refulgent exhibitions of His glory. He can impart to those exhibitions continual growth and enlargement, and all that perpetually progressive augmentation of which they are susceptible. He can do it by His providence, directing, governing, and overruling all the affairs of men, and so bring Himself into view that they shall see His hand, and acknowledge and honor Him as God over all. He can do it by His Spirit, enlightening the minds and subduing the hearts of those who are strangers to the power of His grace, and sanctifying and comforting His own people so that they shall everywhere rejoice in Him, and "exalt His name together." He can do it by His mercies; He can do it by His judgments; He can do it by His ministers; He can do it by His friends and He can do it by His enemies, making all their designs, purposes and efforts either a voluntary or involuntary instrument in promoting His own ends and magnifying His great name.

When men have dishonored Him; when His cause and glory have been lost sight of and forgotten; when His name has been profaned, His altars demolished, the ark of Israel's God carried captive and set up in the temple of idols; when His Church has been covered with sackcloth, and His ministers have stood between the porch and the altar to bewail her desolations; many a time has He thus plucked His right hand out of His bosom, made His arm bare, and "remembered His holy name." And notwithstanding all that He has done, there will yet be brighter illustrations of His glory, and His name be more universally exalted. He shall "endure forever; be continued as long as the sun; and men shall be blessed in Him, and all nations shall call Him blessed."

There is another general inquiry, the answer to which may serve still further to illustrate the import of this petition: Why does this petition hold so high a place in this summary of prayer; and why is it so desirable and important that God's name should be hallowed?

We cannot answer these inquiries as they deserve to be answered. They bring us near the ineffable glory, and make us veil our faces, as in the presence of the God who is invisible. There is nothing of which He Himself is so jealous, nothing which He regards so sensitively, as the glory of His name. We would not have our poor name suffer reproach; much less will the God of heaven allow His honors to be sullied. Rather He is immutably resolved to secure, defend, and advance them, and by all means, and at every sacrifice. The Lord God is a jealous God. He will not give His glory to another. He knows Himself. He forms a just estimate of His own character and station. He cannot but treat Himself according to the just conceptions He has of His own greatness and excellency. He cannot deny Himself, nor can He be indifferent to the manner in which His creatures are affected towards Him. Great and eternal interests depend upon the honors of His name. We shall dwell a few moments upon the reasons which justify these general remarks.

Our Heavenly Father's name and honor are justly great and endeared. It is the greatest, most endeared name in the universe. Angels cannot bear to see it dishonored because He is God their Maker and Sovereign. His children cannot, because He is their Father, and they have all the honorable, honored sentiments of children. The Eternal One, the Mighty God, the Everlasting Father, He who is Himself the beginning, measure, and end of all that exists, and from whom every creature has received all that it is and has, deserves the homage He claims. The Being whose nature, purposes, will, and Word are such as His, is worthy of the hallowed exaltation for which His people are taught to pray. The immense and infinite Deity who is everywhere, and whose being and presence are separated by no distance, and confined by no space, is worthy to dwell in the thoughts, have a throne in the heart, be extolled by the lips, and shine forth in the life of creatures who are enfolded in the arms and carried in the bosom of His infinity! The holy Being, the splendor of whose purity dazzles the sun, and renders heaven itself impure compared with Him, is worthy to be hallowed not only by man who is born of a woman and unclean, but by all the angels of God. The all-powerful God may well command the respect and fear of creatures whose foundation is in the dust, and who dwell in tabernacles of clay. He whose watchful eye equally discerns whatever passes in the thickest darkness and in the clearest light, who knows intuitively all that can be known, and who "destroys the wisdom of the wise, and bringeth to naught the understanding of the prudent," ought not in vain to look down from heaven upon the sons of men to see if they respect His intelligence, and bow humbly before the dictates of His wisdom. The good and gracious God, who loves the weak and guilty inhabitants of this lower world, who bowed His high heavens and took their nature, in that complex nature suffered and died that they might not suffer and die, may well challenge, for His own sake, every expression of grateful homage. Sovereign honors belong, too, to the just God; and earth and heaven should resound with the song of Moses as well as the song of the Lamb.

Why should not His character and conduct appear, as well as be, without a stain? What turpitude and imperfection will be disclosed in the unfoldings of His nature? Why should His excellence be obscured, His glory fade in retirement, His exalted nature wither in solitude, and never shine forth in their appropriate splendor? In a world that lies in wickedness, His holy name has been subjected to the foulest stains; nor will it ever appear in cloudless glory, dissipating the darkness by which it has been enveloped by the ignorance, misconception, and wickedness of men, until it is seen as it is, and is everywhere hallowed as the greatest, the best, and most endeared name.

That God's name should be hallowed is also demanded by the great interests of holiness in our world. Holiness consists in conformity to God. This was the character and image in which man was first created; this the character from which he fell; this is the character in which he is renewed by the Holy Spirit, and in which, once renewed, he perseveres to life eternal. This is the character of heaven. Heaven and earth have but one and the same religion, though they differ in degree; and that religion consists in conformity to the moral character of God as the fruit of His Spirit.

In the economy of nature and grace, there are established laws and uniform connections. Upon nothing does the holiness of creatures so much depend, as its instrumental cause, as the knowledge of God. There can be no more conformity to God in any mind than there is a knowledge of His true character. Truth is the great instrument of conversion to men who are dead in sin, and the great means of sanctification to the converted. And it is by those very means by which men hallow the name of God, and by which He hallows His own name; it is by those means that the truth is brought home to their own bosoms and achieves its greatest conquests. It is in the intelligent and devout utterance of the petition, "Hallowed be Thy name," that the soul catches a portion of that heavenly spirit which she ascribes to her great heavenly Parent, and which she thus desires may be every where exhibited and made known. It is thus that she rises to the character of that favored and hallowed society, who "all come in the unity of the faith, and of the knowledge of the Son of God, into the measure of the stature of the fullness of Christ," and "with open face, beholding as in a glass the glory of the Lord, are changed into the same image, from glory to glory, even as by the Spirit of the Lord." As well might we enjoy without aliment, or vigor without exercise, as spirituality of mind, in the neglect of the means of spirituality. We become enriched by the communications of heavenly grace, only as the storehouse of our spiritual perceptions and thoughts is receiving new accessions. Not until the good treasure of the heart is supplied from these divine sources does it become a sacred repository of good things. It is here we find the materials and excitements of holy and devout affections. Here is the intimacy and delight of intercourse with God. Here we bewail and mortify our worst affections, and give scope to our best ones. Here we become acquainted with ourselves, our state, our temper, our dispositions, our character, and, under the influence of the sanctifying Spirit, become more humble, more watchful, more sensible of our dependence on the grace of God, and more devoted to His glory. How many millions among the perfected spirits of the just, and millions more on their way to that world of bliss, who connect their purest recollections and their most purifying hopes and anticipations, with hallowing and seeing hallowed the great and endeared name of their Father who is in heaven!

It is in and by these contemplations, that the holiness of heaven itself is progressive and perpetual. Take away from the bosom of these celestial inhabitants those strong affections which arise from their perceptions of the divine nature; separate from their present character those deep, adoring, and grateful emotions which flow forth from their perpetually enlarging views of the adorable Godhead, and most sensibly do you abate their intense and high admiration of His infinite excellence, and the growing ecstasy of their everlasting song.

Inseparable from these suggestions also is the thought that the happiness of creatures requires that God's name should be hallowed. The time was when there was nothing in existence save the infinite God. No more is He the beginning and source of all creatures than of all created good. He has assigned to every one of the human family His sphere, His mode, and His period of existence till they all return to their final destiny, the dust to the earth whence it was taken, the spirit to God who gave it. When his period of existence on the earth is ended, then that great day of eternity will begin, when all the holy will be gathered together, and return to Him who made and redeemed them, to rest forever in the bosom of His love, the seat of blessedness, the center of repose. He is the supreme happiness and end of man, the source and fullness of all his joy. The world is made for man, but man himself is made for God. The soul which God has given him, no sensual delights can content or satisfy; it breathes after purer joys, and happiness more enduring. Nor can it be satisfied except with God Himself. To know God, to love God, to possess and enjoy God, is the end to which his immortal existence aspires, and without which it is impossible for it to be a happy, joyous existence. It is restless until it rests in Him, joyless until it becomes partaker of His joy.

And how do we become partakers of His joy except by seeing His nature and perfections unfolded, His name hallowed, and ourselves delighting and happy in these manifestations of His glory! There is something in the divine nature, not merely for the employment of our intellectual powers, but for the gratification of our most exalted and spiritual affections. Let God be brought into view, and a holy mind will be happy; let God be withdrawn and it is miserable. The happiest moment of the Christian's life is when he enjoys the most enlarged and most impressive views of God, and dwells with adoring wonder on His boundless and unsearchable perfections. Nothing can make him miserable while the glory of the divine character, and the light of the divine countenance, is lifted up upon him. Everywhere, without this, there remains a fearful blank, a chasm which the created universe cannot fill. Here the understanding is satisfied, conscience is at peace through atoning blood, and the heart finds repose and joy. The understanding is gratified with truths into which angels desire to look; the heart is attracted by love that is above all other love; the conscience, though more sensitive, is at the same time more tranquil; and the very imagination feeds on all that is sublime and beautiful, because it is great and lovely. The tear of affliction is wiped away. Sorrow and sighing there find their true solace. Darkness is chased by light, and the streams that embitter are forgotten in the joys that flow.

Just in the measure in which God's name is hallowed by us and by our fellow men are these sources of happiness found within our own bosoms, and diffused around us. The Christian is greatly comforted with the thought that his heavenly Father's name will be hallowed, because he discovers in this assurance the plentitude of joy to himself, and this barren and otherwise joyless creation. When worn out with pains and labors, when sick with the agitating excitements of earth, he forgets his cares and griefs as he goes to bow before the throne and say, "Our Father, which art in heaven, hallowed be Thy name!" It is quietude to his fears, balm to his bleeding heart, peace to all its strifes, and hope and joy amid all its depressions, if that name is but hallowed. If created happiness is to be estimated from the purity, sublimity, and sufficiency of its source, from the greatness of its joys and from the extent of its duration, here its source is the infinite God, its joys the delights which flow from seeing Him and being like Him, its duration His own boundless eternity.

Thus dear are the name and honor of God to His people. Thus true is it that holiness is the creature's greatest glory, sin his shame and everlasting disgrace. Thus true is it that God Himself is the soul's highest good, and that those who glorify Him will enjoy Him forever. They will enter into and rejoice in His joy, shine in His splendor; and in a little while, unspeakably more than they have honored Him, be honored by Him, and receive from His hands their unfading crown, their robes of immortality. It should be our desire above all things that His name should have the glory come what will, that His name stand forth in untarnished, augmented luster.

Woe to the man who cannot say from the heart, "Hallowed be Thy name." And woe to him who utters this request, yet makes no scruple of dishonoring the name of God, profaning it at heart, and bringing his contempt of it to God's altars! Let it be the reader's concern that his heavenly Father's glory is the object dearest to his heart. Let His name be hallowed, beloved, and declared, and its sacred impulse felt. There is no end so worthy of God to designate, or man to pursue. Honored He will be; and amid all the disorder of this world He will bring light out of darkness and make crooked things straight. His ardent and mighty affections concentrate in this great end, and "the zeal of the Lord of hosts will perform this." Jehovah has sworn by Himself, "As I live, the whole earth shall be filled with My glory!" Creation, providence, and redemption shall honor Him. All His purposes shall be unfolded; all His character shall be made known, and His glory shall never cease to shine till it fills the earth as the waters fill the sea.

Delightful, inexpressibly delightful thoughts are these, as we look over this disordered world. Everything was made for God; and was not man made for Him? Were the pebble and the worm made for Him? Were the mountains, the seas, and the rivers made for Him? Were the atmosphere and the light, the cattle upon a thousand hills, all the fowls of the mountains, summer and winter, and seed time and harvest made for Him? They all fulfill their destiny, and will not men fulfill a destiny so much more exalted than theirs? Reader, you were made for God. Why then will you not acknowledge Him as the great All in all, and welcome His reign in you and over you forever? Why shall not His honor be your honor, His kingdom your kingdom, His riches your riches, and His joy your joy? There is a silent eloquence in the heavens and in the earth, as they fulfill their courses and praise their mighty Maker, making its appeal to you to glorify God in your bodies and spirits, which are His. There is affecting solicitude revealed in that sacred volume, above the eloquence of nature, when it says, "Oh, that men would praise the Lord for His goodness, for His wonderful works to the children of men!" There is a tenderness from the cross that says, "Father! I will that they also whom Thou hast given Me may be with Me where I am, that they may behold My glory which Thou hast given Me." And there is a universal appeal, like the voice of many waters, and as the voice of mighty thunderings, from every creature which is in heaven and on the earth, and under the earth, and such as are in the sea, and all that are in them, themselves saying, "Blessing, and honor, and glory, and power, be unto Him that sitteth upon the throne, and unto the Lamb, forever and ever!" and giving utterance and emphasis to the demand, "Who shall not fear Thee, O Lord, and glorify Thy name? For Thou only art holy!"

Chapter 5

The Kingdom of God on the Earth
"Thy Kingdom Come"

There is a wisdom to be consulted beyond our wisdom, a glory beyond our glory, and an interest beyond our interest. Hence the petition, "Hallowed be Thy name." The next great object is the accomplishment of God's purposes of mercy to our world; purposes as far exceeding our thoughts as His capacity exceeds our own. In the same measure in which we desire that His name should be hallowed will the prayer of our hearts be, "Thy kingdom come."

When the solitary Christian enters into his closet, shuts his door, and prays to his Father who is in secret, he utters no request more fervently than this. The dwelling places of Mount Zion, on which God creates a fire and a smoke, everywhere offering up their thousand sacrifices, repeat no petition more uniformly. The laborious minister of the gospel in Christian lands, and the faithful missionary of the cross among the heathen, amid all that is alternately encouraging and disheartening in their prospects, find no nearer or more exalted communion with God than when they bow at His footstool in the true purport and comprehensiveness of the request and say, "Thy kingdom come." The Church of God on earth, in all her prayers, in all her songs, and in all her instructions and ordinances, utters the spirit, and urges the importance of this petition. Nay, the great atoning, interceding Savior, who ascended to His Father and our Father, to His God and our God, is still uttering these words, and with the same tenderness and emphasis with which He taught them to His disciples: "Thy kingdom come." And blessed be His name, "He which testifieth these things saith, 'Surely I come quickly. Amen,' Even so, come, Lord Jesus!"

It is of some consequence to have just conceptions of the import of the phrase, "The kingdom of God." The whole universe is the empire of Jehovah; the range of His government is limited by nothing but the vast circle of universal existence. "The Lord hath prepared His throne in the heavens, and His kingdom ruleth over all." "Thine, O Lord, is the greatness, and the glory, and the majesty; for all that is in the heaven and earth is Thine." "Thine is the kingdom, O Lord! Thou art exalted above all; Thou reignest over all!"

This universal empire has not been maintained without a struggle. There have been, and still are, rivals for the throne, to some extent successful in their rivalship. The time was when the King of the universe not only controlled this earth and all the planetary worlds, but ruled in the hearts of every order of intelligences; angels and men cheerfully recognized His authority and celebrated His praise. No records inform us how long this universal dominion continued thus undisturbed. One mournful fact we have ascertained: in the far distant ages of the past, there was a revolt, a revolt in heaven, a revolt among the angels of God. Great multitudes combined in this treasonable enterprise, "left their first habitation," and were cast out on some remote continent, some lower region of the universe, where they set up a kingdom of their own which still exists, and is the great rival power to the throne and monarchy of God.

Among the early successes of this revolt was the fatal seduction of the human family. Placed, as our first parents were, under a law, the penalty of which was death to themselves and their posterity, the prince of darkness did not fail to see that if he prevailed in enticing them from their allegiance to the Most High, he would, by this act, bring sin and ruin upon their descendants. He did entice them; and the penalty for this first offence has been visited upon this fallen race. The deed was done that hoisted the floodgates of iniquity, and poured its desolation through every successive generation of men. Henceforth men began their existence in the moral likeness of their fallen parents, and were the children of disobedience and wrath. A kingdom was established and grew that breathed nothing but rebellion against the Most High. The great adversary seemed to triumph. From that hour, he has been pushing his conquests, from age to age, and from one end of the world to the other, in some minds holding a partial sway, in others absolute and entire dominion; in some lands with repulsed power, in others with unrestrained power.

In such a world, and amid these conflicts, the God of heaven has set up a kingdom in which He feels the deepest interest, because His own honor is staked upon its successes, and because it is identified with those high interests of moral rectitude of which He is the Vindicator and Guardian. In the purpose and grace of its Founder, this kingdom was set up from everlasting, or ever the earth was. It began in fact to exist immediately after the fall of our first parents. Its beginning was small, but here and there a few enlisted under its banners, while the great mass of men remained the vassals of the prince of darkness. In this state of depression, sometimes more and sometimes less comprehensive, it continued during the patriarchal, Mosaic, and prophetic ages. Other kingdoms rose and fell; but this, small as it was, held on its way, and though its glory was obscured, it was still a light amid surrounding darkness.

But the time had come when an important epoch was to

give greater character and prominence to this kingdom. During that long and humiliating exile of the ancient Church in Babylon, a distinguished prophet was raised up who predicted the overthrow of her captors and foretold the rise and fall of the Grecian and Persian empires; and in his anticipations of the extent and durability of the Roman power, he uses this remarkable language: "In those days shall the God of heaven set up a kingdom, which shall never be destroyed; and the kingdom shall not be left to other people, but it shall break in pieces, and consume all these kingdoms, and it shall stand forever." After the Roman empire was established, and amid the glory of the Augustan age, the distinguished personage on whose shoulders the government of this kingdom was to rest made His appearance in our world; the predicted Messiah was born. About thirty years later, and under the reign of Tiberius Caesar, He was crucified and slain, rose from the dead, ascended up into heaven, established His kingdom on the earth upon a broader basis, and began to reign in the power of His own truth and grace. And this is what is meant in the Scriptures by the phrase, "The kingdom of God." It is the reign of Christ, the empire of the Messiah as David's Son and Lord, on the earth.

We shall have still clearer views of this kingdom by specifying some of its great features. It possesses very remarkable characteristics, and is unlike every other kingdom.

It is emphatically distinguished by the character and authority of its great Prince. "Unto us a child is born, unto us a Son is given, and His name shall be called Wonderful, Counselor, the Mighty God, the Everlasting Father, the Prince of Peace." In every view, He is truly called "Wonderful." He is the mysterious Word who was in the beginning with God, and was God, who created all things, both visible and invisible, whether they are thrones, dominions, principalities, or powers. He possesses inherent and high born honors. His personal glory shines forth as "the glory of the only begotten of the Father, full of grace and truth." He is the Seed of the woman, and yet is the Son of the Highest. He stood before the bar of earthly princes, and yet had all the kingdoms and empires of this world at His disposal. He "came not to be ministered unto, but to minister," yet "hath He on His vesture and on His thigh a name written, 'King of kings, and Lord of lords.' " His palace was a stable, His court and retinue a few fishermen and tax-gatherers, yet angels were His attendants and the heaven of heavens His dwelling place. His crown was a wreath of thorns, His scepter a reed, and His throne a cross; yet in His hand is the scepter that rules the nations, on His head are many crowns, and His throne is the right hand of Majesty on high.

Nothing can be more absolute than the authority which Christ exercises in His own kingdom; nor will He consent to exercise any other than that which is perfectly uncontrolled. At all times, under all circumstances, and in its whole procedure and administration, this kingdom is subjected to Him as its great and sole Monarch. Its common law and its positive statutes may be prescribed by no earthly and secular power. In no one particular may His decisions be departed from. No alliance with any of the empires of earth may be arranged and determined that shall call into question, or in the least degree limit, His exclusive right to rule in His own house. Its form, its officers, its worship, and its powers and privileges, are all derived from Him, exist through Him and for Him, and are all to be exercised in accordance with His will. No indifference on the one hand, nor bitterness of persecution on the other; no rich endowment and no depressing poverty; no human traditions, however venerable for age, or consecrated by usage and custom; no decisions of counsels or of popes, however arrogant their claims to infallibility; no Christian fathers, no daring pretenses of an aspiring priesthood in any one department of this kingdom, may release its members from His paramount authority, impair His right to be heard as their Prophet and Guide, and to be obeyed as their King and Head. No revolutions of time, no change in the relations this kingdom sustains to the kingdoms of this world, can modify its relation to Him who alone has the keys of the house of David, and sits upon the throne. It is more than all human thrones, councils, laws, and decisions are worth, to bind what the Lord Jesus has not bound, or loose what He has not loosed. The community over which He reigns is a kingdom because it is a monarchy; it has but one Ruler, and no vice-regents; its ruler is God in the person of the Lord Jesus.

Another peculiarity of this kingdom will be found in the principles by which it is administered. Justice and judgment are the habitation of God's throne; these are the great principles on which it is built and stands firm; they are the place, the basis, and the foundation on which it rests. Yet is there a wondrous combination and assemblage of the divine attributes in the administration of divine justice, as dispensed in this kingdom. "Mercy and truth are met together; righteousness and peace have kissed each other." These apparently jarring perfections of the divine nature are here reconciled, and brought into a state of most endeared harmony. Man's redemption from sin and hell by Jesus Christ presents to the contemplation of the universe the union of principles which seem to be absolutely irreconcilable. That perfect and unerring rectitude which is an essential perfection of the divine nature, which is without blemish and without change, which by its love of holiness and hatred of sin is the strong support and unsleeping guardian of holiness in the universe, and which is armed with such terrors against the guilty—instead of driving its rebellious subjects from the face of the throne into the lake of fire is here made to combine with that heavenly mercy which stoops to sinners, and pardons, justifies, sanctifies, and advances them to the adoption of sons. In the administration of this kingdom there are no divine attributes that are sustained at the expense of others; all are equal, have equally honored claims, and give unequalled beauty and luster to the whole character of its reigning Sovereign. His justice receives new honors from His mercy. His mercy receives exaltation it never could have received had it not been thus exalted by His justice. And in this pre-eminently consists the force and excellence of His claims upon the hearts of His subjects. His very law is clothed with new power by the grace that brings salvation, because it here has demands that are beyond the demands of a purely legal administration: demands of grace, laws of love and mercy. This is the great principle of the divine kingdom, and to this great instrumentality must be attributed its successes and triumphs. Nay, this was its origin; it never had existed but for the condescension of the "Word made flesh," and His mediatorial office in bringing into one the justice that punishes and the grace that saves. The principles by which this kingdom is administered, therefore, are altogether peculiar. They have no sympathy with the principles of earthly princes; it is a kingdom not of this world. Its laws evidence how widely different it is from all earthly kingdoms. It speaks the same language to all its subjects, and it is alike adapted to them all, whatever their different shades of character or outward condition.

Principles which thus originate with the heart of the Deity are fitted to address themselves to the hearts of men. Hence one peculiarity of the laws of this kingdom is the fact that they are spiritual, and go beyond the exterior man. They aim at the heart. They require more than an outward respect and submission; their object is to secure a heart-felt, affectionate, and cheerful obedience. They enthrone the Prince and Savior over the thoughts; they make Him the God of the affections, the Lord of the will. That great law, so endless in its ramifications, "Thou shalt love the Lord thy God with all thy heart, and thy neighbor as thyself," is the standard of character, the great rule of action in the divine kingdom. It is one which never changes, and is in full force and obligation through illimitable ages. The service it requires is a reasonable service, the offspring of an enlightened faith, and such as is becoming man to offer and God to accept. No right-hearted man ever complained of the laws of the divine kingdom as being too strict, too extended, or too spiritual. Rather he acquiesces in them, gives them his warmest attachment, and though they may do violence to flesh and blood, and urge to laborious duties and painful sacrifices, yet is it no part of his character to impugn their excellence.

Another peculiarity of this kingdom is found in the character of its subjects. The subjects of this kingdom are they who are redeemed by the blood of its Prince, and sanctified by His Spirit; they are those who have diligently weighed and pondered His precepts; who have habitual reference to His rule, and give it a place in the ordinary current of their thoughts; who are impressed with a deep sense of their obligations, accompanied with a sincere resolution of implicit and unreserved obedience, and who are inspired with a love to His law after the inner man. They possess a congeniality of mind with the spirit and tenor of God's Word, while their practical compliance with it is the effect of the love of God shed abroad in their hearts, and of that inward vital principle of faith in Jesus Christ imparted by the Holy Spirit. The Scriptures describe them as "born of God." This work of the Spirit is the seal of God on the heart of His servants, and the distinguishing feature in their character. Their life is hidden with Christ in God. This union to Him is the source of their holiness, the secret of their strength, the glory of their hopes. This character possesses all the subjects of this kingdom, in all ages of the world, and throughout all its extent it is essentially the same character everywhere. Wherever this character exists, there are the subjects of this kingdom. They are patriarchs, prophets, apostles, martyrs, and confessors; they are Christian men, Christian women, and Christian children, all over the earth. Though naturally destitute of holiness, and under the entire dominion of a depraved heart, their internal views and affections are so essentially changed that old things are passed away and all things are become new. They have a spiritual discerning of spiritual things; they love what they formerly did not love, and hate what they did not formerly hate. They are those who place God on the throne, and take their proper place at His footstool; and though they have no reason for self-exultation, and cause for glorying only in the cross of Christ, yet very many of them are men of whom the world is not worthy, the excellent of the earth, and the glory of the nations. They form a distinct communion amid this world's vast population, often a little flock; but they are the salt of the earth, the light of the world, a peculiar people, who show forth the praises of Him who bought them, and because He bought them, brought them forth from the kingdom of Satan into the kingdom of His dear Son.

Another peculiarity of this kingdom, therefore, consists in its benevolent and hallowed influence. Depraved as the world is, its great security under God is in the practical influence of this divine kingdom. But for this, there would be no reverence for the truth of God among men. The subjects of this kingdom are His witnesses; their hearts, their families, and their altars are the selected depositories of His truth. They themselves are living epistles of it, known and read of all men. Exterminate this kingdom, and the nations would go back to the night of paganism, with none to guide their feet in the way of peace; this earth would again be immerged in darkness, and in the shadow of death. But for this kingdom, there would be no reverence for God Himself, and none for His law. Errors, infidelity, and ungodliness would become everywhere so rife in the earth, and the corrupt propensities and passions of men would so throw off their wonted restraints, as to call for the interposing judgments of the insulted Majesty of heaven. The times would be calamitous because men would become degenerate, and God would be angry. Occupying the hills, and entrenched by the strongholds of Zion, this kingdom forms the only barrier against the swelling, menacing tide of human wretchedness; it plants firm and lifts high its standard for truth and right, for religion and virtue, for order, safety, and happiness. It stands alone; and has the courage to do so, in view of opposition however formidable, and sacrifices however great.

Another of the distinctions of this kingdom is that it is a happy kingdom. Those who are out of it are in a state of rebellion against their rightful Sovereign; they are contending with God—who is mighty to save and mighty to destroy—and reason, conscience, and all the principles of that government which its mighty Monarch has established forbid that they should be happy. On the other hand, those who are within it, though they may be no favorites with the world, are the favorites of Heaven. Whatever else they forego, they do not forego the favor of God, nor their enjoyment of Him, nor any of the sources of true blessedness. Nothing earthly can give them the happiness they seek. The kingdom of God has come to them as suffering, perishing men, with the abundance of its light, the plentitude of its pardons, and the redundancy of its grace. The malady and the misery which consisted in their departure from God are healed by their being restored. They have now peace with God, with whom they were once at war; peace with His government, to which they were once hostile; peace with themselves, whose bosoms were once like the troubled sea; peace with their fellow men, once hateful and hating one another; and all made sure by Him who is the God of peace, and through Him who is the Prince of Peace. Peace is one of the great characteristics of this kingdom. "Prince of Peace" is the name of its King. Under His reign the mountains shall bring peace to the people, and the little hills by righteousness. He "maketh wars to cease unto the ends of the earth." He is that Sun of righteousness who rises with healing in His wings. He shall "come down like rain upon the mown grass; as showers that water the earth; all nations shall call Him blessed; all people shall obtain joy and gladness, and sorrow and sighing shall flee away."

O scenes surpassing fable, and yet true!
Scenes of accomplished bliss! Which who can see
Though but in distant prospect, and not feel
His soul refreshed with foretaste of the joy!

The only remaining characteristic of this kingdom on which I shall dwell is its perpetuity. It is a kingdom which shall never be destroyed; it shall not be left to other people; it shall stand forever. "Of this kingdom," said the angel Gabriel to Mary, "there shall be no end." The gates of hell shall not prevail against it. The heavens and the earth shall pass away, but the words of its divine Founder shall never pass away. Other kingdoms may be celebrated for their wealth and splendor, for the fame of their emperors, and the extent of their conquests; but they live only on the page of history. Other kingdoms are immortalized in song because they may have been the birthplace of freedom or the favored habitations of genius; yet in a little while you look in vain for one remaining trace of their proud glory. Their princes die like men, while the vast empires over which they reigned carry within them the elements of their own destruction. The kingdom of God shall outvie and outlive them all; it carries within it no elements of destruction, but rather the secret of its own perpetuity. Its origin and the method by which it was acquired, the principles by which it is administered, and the immortality and universal presence of its Founder are the sure pledge of its eternal progress. Its great Founder Himself promises to be with this society of His redeemed to the end of the world. The kingdom which He founded by His humiliation He will not abandon now that He is exalted to the right hand of the Majesty on high. "He must reign until all enemies are put under His feet." His empire has been advancing for centuries in defiance of all the powers of darkness; and though its enemies may be many, and subtle and powerful; and though the work to be accomplished in carrying it forward is great, yet shall it advance to the utter subversion and ruin of the powers combined against it, till "the kingdoms of this world become the kingdoms of our Lord and His Christ, and He shall reign forever and ever."

Such is the kingdom of our Father who is in heaven. Lift up your eyes, you who are the children of God, and survey its glories. They are not the wealth, honors, and pleasures of this exterior universe which it brings to you, but inward blessedness, holier joys, and an imperishable inheritance. It is not meat and drink, but "righteousness, peace, and joy in the Holy Ghost." The full glories of that kingdom are indeed yet to be revealed. You have the earnest of them in actual possession. The kingdom of God is within you; and though the crown and the scepter as yet await you in eternity, the day is not far distant when, with the spirits of just men made perfect, and the unfallen and immortal princes of this kingdom, you shall take your place with cherubim and seraphim, and stand in the presence of God. Though still in your minority, and even the infancy of your adoption, yet are you heirs of God, and joint-heirs with Jesus Christ. Many a weary day may be appointed you of conflict with your enemies, and the enemies of your Prince, but the contest will ere long be over and the victory won. Let, then, the expectants of such a kingdom demean themselves in a way befitting their inheritance, and worthy of their allegiance to such a Prince.

There are those who are still in a state of rebellion against this King of Zion. Such persons cannot say from the heart, "Thy kingdom come." They are as yet under the dominion of another master, and belong to a kingdom that must be subverted and destroyed. The exalted Messiah, in terrible majesty, is even now executing judgment upon His enemies, thereby imparting a new impulse to His own glorious reign. Be wise now, therefore; be instructed, you kings and people of the earth. "Serve the Lord with fear, and rejoice with trembling. Kiss the Son, lest He be angry, and ye perish from the way, when His wrath is kindled but a little." An awful state is that of an unconverted sinner. He is a rebel against the best kingdom; he is Satan's subject and servant. Think of this, you who forget God; think of it while it is called today. If the Prince and Savior has no throne within your heart; if His Spirit does not influence, nor His laws govern you; if you have no holiness and no peace in His salvation, you are still under the power of the prince of darkness and the god of this world. Yet is it an unspeakably precious truth that you are still a prisoner of hope; that preparatory to the kingdom of glory hereafter is the day and kingdom of grace here. Be sure of this, then, that the kingdom of God has come nigh unto you. Whosoever will may enter in. The gates are not shut, either night or day. The Spirit and the Bride say, "Come." They open wide its portals, and point you to its treasures and its throne. Come, enter in. Every subject is a king in that kingdom; every head wears a crown of righteousness; in every heart there is fullness of joy.

Chapter 6

The Means of Extending God's Kingdom
"Thy Kingdom Come"

The kingdom of God, as we have exhibited its nature and characteristics in the previous chapter, is His spiritual reign over the minds of men. Occupying, as it does, the thoughts and counsels of the Eternal Mind, before the heavens were stretched out or the foundations of the earth were laid, it still forms His great master purpose. It is destined to advance; but the inquiry is one of interest: How, and by what means, is its advancement to be secured?

Its conquests are not physical, nor political, nor military conquests, but spiritual victories, and are achieved by a spiritual armor. There are preparatory measures by which the minds of men are rendered accessible to its influences. There is an intimate connection between the system of providence and the method of grace. One of the selected and ordained means of advancing the kingdom of God ever has been the revolutions and conduct of His own mighty providence. It is the purpose of infinite love that this kingdom shall ultimately absorb every other interest, and, in accomplishing this purpose, He must necessarily extend His government beyond those established laws of nature which constitute a general providence. He must exercise a particular providence over all human affairs; without this prerogative His mediatorial office would be incomplete. If the nations are given unto Him for an inheritance, the arrangements of His providence must be such as to give His truth access to their minds; and when they have become identified with His kingdom, these arrangements must be such as to render Him their effectual guardian.

His providence, in ways unseen as well as seen, prepares the way for His gospel, and is the appointed precursor to herald its approach. The history of the past, as well as events that are taking place under our own observation, abundantly show how the many overturnings in the affairs of men serve the purpose of His mediatorial reign. The enterprises of those thus employed as God's instruments may be unhallowed enterprises; they may originate with pride, and be prompted by love of power; they may aim solely at wealth, conquest, or revenge; but though they mean it for evil, God means it for good. Even the sword of the conqueror receives its commission from Him who purposes to follow it with the sword of His Spirit. Walls that have rendered millions impervious to His truth have been battered down by men whom He has raised up, and qualified, directed, and prospered for His own ends. His providence has many a time riveted chains upon the necks of His enemies so that His people might go free, and, on the other hand, has knocked off those chains so that His people may enjoy the common liberty of His enemies. When science has been pursuing her researches; when the arts have been following up their improvements on the sea and on the land, and amid all the elements of nature; when men of wealth and men of toil have been pushing their enterprises through the rock and mountainous wilderness, and have joined sea to sea and shore to shore, an unseen but almighty hand has been guiding their bold and hazardous undertakings, so that His way may be known, and His saving health among all nations.

As it has been, so it will be. Many a valley is to be exalted, and many a mountain laid low; many a crooked way is to be made straight, and many a stream to be dried up, so that the way for the Redeemer's conquests may be prepared and the ransomed of the Lord may pass over. Empire after empire is yet to be overturned; the lofty are to be brought low and the lowly are to be lifted up; great and mighty movements are to be looked for in the world and periods of disastrous revolution to the powers of darkness so that the God of Israel may make to Himself a name, and the ark of His strength be exalted on the earth. The providence of God is the expositor, as well as the precursor and the executor, of His purposes of mercy. The origin and progress, the decline and fall, of nations and governments are all under His control who "worketh all things after the counsel of His own will." His counsels record their history; in His calendar are marked the hours of their advancement and their pride. He opens the seals of the book where the time is noted when He shall overturn them, in order to give place to that kingdom for which all other things were made. "He shall remove the diadem, and take off the crown; exalt him that is low, and abase him that is high; He shall overturn, overturn, and overturn, and it shall be no more until He comes whose right it is, and He will give it Him."

In addition to these preparatory arrangements, there are moral instrumentalities by which this kingdom is to be advanced. In those movements of divine providence that are directed and overruled to the coming of Christ's kingdom, men, so far as regards the ends God is aiming at, are, for the most part, the passive and even the unconscious instruments. Yet has man an active part to perform in advancing the interests of this kingdom. He is a subaltern in this spiritual warfare; he is to occupy the post assigned him; he has the means of both aggression and defense. They are not unhallowed principles which he is warranted to make use of, nor are they sustained by unhallowed motives. They are not the power of the secular arm, enforcing the edicts of the Church. They are not fines and forfeitures, fire and sword, racks and chains, banishment and the dungeon. Nor are they entangling alliances between the Church and the State, the civil establishments of religion, the wisely invented checks and balances of the wily politician. Nor do they partake of the nature of those human devices in the worship of God, which have been so abundantly superceded to the simplicity that is in Christ. They are not the intercession of departed saints, nor the flames of purgatory, nor the merit of penitence, nor works of supererogation, nor the celibacy of the clergy, nor the scarlet robes of the priesthood, nor any of the endless superstitions whereby the man of sin has deceived the nations. Nor are they the subtitles of philosophy, the speculations of reason, the pride and ostentation of unsanctified learning and eloquence. Nor are they the disingenuousness and crooked policy of a faithless ministry that would please men. The means are few and simple, efficacious, and of divine appointment. They are the truth and love of the gospel; the light, the power of truth; the ardor, the fire of love.

They are the Word of the living God, published to all nations, and sustained by the institutions, example, and influence of His Church. These are, indeed, means which seem inadequate to the end because they are so simple and so few. "The kingdom of God cometh not with observation." The stone spoken of by the prophet Daniel, which was emblematic of this kingdom, was "cut out of the mountain without hands." Like the temple at Jerusalem, "neither hammer nor axe, nor any tool of iron, is heard in the house while it is building." They are means which address themselves to the intellectual and moral nature of man; which make their appeal to his reason, his conscience, and his heart; which speak to the soul on the authority of their Author; which are as silent in their influence as the dew of heaven; balmy as the droppings of mercy from the wings of the angel flying through the midst of heaven, diffusive and life-giving as is the Sun of Righteousness, when He rises with healing in his beams.

The simple preaching of Christ and Him crucified occupies the first place among the great instrumentalities by which the kingdom of darkness is to be overcome, and men are to be brought into the kingdom of God.

The pulpit must stand acknowledged,
While the world shall stand,
The most important and effectual guard,
Support, and ornament of virtue's cause.

"The words that I speak unto you," said the Savior, "they are spirit and they are life." Whatever that word contains; whatever of God in His glory and His humiliation; whatever of man, fallen and redeemed; whatever of the pity of heaven for the apostasy of earth; whatever glad tidings of great joy there are in His obedience unto death, and in a gratuitous justification by faith in His blood; intelligently, faithfully, and affectionately exhibited, and urged upon the conscience by all the sanctions of the eternal world—this is the instrumentality by which the wonderful changes spoken of in the Scriptures are yet to be effected in this world, and the kingdom of God is to gain its decisive victories. Heavenly truth and heavenly love are to accomplish these conquests; heavenly truth, because true piety is everywhere conformity to the truth of God, nor can it exist save where that truth is perceived and loved; heavenly love, because there is no other way of carrying a hostile world than by drawing it with cords of love, those bands of a man. In portraying the successes of His empire, the Spirit of God addresses the King of Zion in the following language: "Gird Thy sword upon Thy thigh, O most mighty, with Thy glory and Thy majesty. And in Thy majesty ride prosperously because of truth, meekness, and righteousness; and Thy right hand shall teach Thee terrible things. Thine arrows are sharp in the hearts of the king's enemies, whereby the people fall under Thee." Mark the means of His conquests, the weapons by which His foes become a conquered yet a willing people, and while they submit to His power, cheerfully and gladly bow at His footstool! They are truth, meekness, and righteousness. This is the "rod of His strength" which He sends out of Zion; these the arrows which perforate and transform the heart.

Another of the means by which this kingdom is advanced is the religious education of the young. There is no greater evidence of the importance to be attached to His means of advancing the reign of God in the hearts of men than the fact that, in the dispensations of both His natural and moral government, God has so closely connected the character and destiny of the child with that of the parent. The covenant with the first father of our race in paradise, the covenant with Noah as the father of the new world, and the covenant with Abraham as the head of the Hebrew nation and the father of all them that believe, confirmed by its impressive seal, furnish affecting proofs of the reality and importance of this great principle, pervading all the varieties of administration in the kingdom of grace.

The Scriptures explicitly teach us that the great design of heavenly wisdom in the institution of the domestic relations, and the organization of the social state, protected as they are by so many sanctions of the most solemn kind, is the moral and religious culture of the rising race. Alluding to the origin of the human family from one pair, the prophet demands, "Did He not make one? And wherefore one? That He might seek a godly seed." There is nothing in which the interests of piety have a deeper stake than these hallowed relations. The whole face and character of human society, and the condition of the church, receive their impression from the character of the rising generation. The religious training of the infantile and youthful mind, though not the exclusive channel, constitutes the selected channel in which the grace of God is wont to flow. The neglect or careless performance of this duty is an unfailing token for evil. Give the adversary the education of the rising generation, and the world will be overrun with a seed of evildoers. There is no time for sowing the seeds of knowledge and grace like the springtime of human life. If the child is neglected, unless some unpromised and unlooked for interposition severs the effect from the case, the man is lost. It is comparatively easy to purify the fountain, but when the streams become diffused and extended they are beyond your reach.

Confirmed obduracy in sin does not belong to the earlier periods of life; a seared conscience is seldom, if ever, found in the bosom of the young. A little child is never the creature of sensuality; nor do care and perplexity so embarrass and enchain the youthful mind as to choke the Word. Faith, hope, and prayer hover, with the deepest interest and highest promise, not over the aged, but the young. The Holy Spirit, the gentle Dove of Heaven, forsakes the rugged bosom which has long been the seat of stormy passions to dwell in the more peaceful and tranquil heart of the devout child.

In those portions of the earth, and in those periods of the world, in which the kingdom of God has been most rapidly extended, it began its advances in the hearts of the young. The great mass of those whose piety has been eminent in the world, as well as the great mass of those who have been most eminent as preachers of the gospel, together with those whom God has honored as the reformers of a corrupt and degenerate age, and the successful missionaries of the cross among the heathen, have sprung from a godly ancestry, and have been trained up in the way in which they should go. There is no more cheering indication of the advancement of God's kingdom on the earth than when youthful converts are multiplied as the drops of the dew. It is a delightful prospect, as the older and more withered trees of righteousness die away, to behold the younger and more vigorous plants shoot up and occupy their places. Blessed is that youthful generation by whom the kingdom of God is thus advanced; and blessed also is that risen generation which is preparing a righteous seed to perform this blessed work!

We do not deprecate other agencies in this great work. We honor the press and the institutions of learning, but they owe their elevating and purifying influence to the Bible, the ministry, and the Church of God. They have accomplished little else than to mislead and corrupt where they are not under a Christian influence. But while these are means of God's appointment, and correspond with the nature of that kingdom which they are designed to promote; and while they possess an evident and strong adaptation to secure its advancement; there is another power by which its advancement is secured—I mean the effectual working of the Holy Spirit. There is no natural tendency in the individual mind, nor in larger associations of minds, to yield to the influences of God's truth, however clearly and impressively exhibited. His truth furnishes but the material, the instrument, the medium by which a superadded and higher power operates on the understanding and heart. In relation to all the means that are adopted for the extension of the Redeemer's kingdom, it may never be forgotten that it is "not by might, nor by power, but by the Spirit of God." Truth enlightens the understanding, and thus presents before the mind the objects of gracious affections; it convinces the conscience, and thus awakens fear and apprehensions; it imparts a sense of obligation, and thus leaves men without excuse in their alienation from God; it fixes powerful associations and presents the strongest inducements to piety in the minds of men who see it as it is, and thus supplies the motives to holiness—but more than this it cannot perform. "Neither is he that planteth anything, neither he that watereth, but God that giveth the increase." Our confidence in the advancement of the Redeemer's kingdom is in the promise. "The Comforter, the Holy Ghost, shall abide with you forever." He alone gives the truth its saving efficacy. "We have this treasure in earthen vessels, that the excellency of the power may be of God and not of us."

Much is indeed gained by those overturnings of divine providence by which the way is prepared for the gospel to have access to the minds of men; more is accomplished by the actual diffusion of the Scriptures in every land, and the dispersion of an instructive and faithful ministry, everywhere dispensing to listening millions the words of eternal life. Still more is effected by the faithful and devout efforts of the Church for the rising generation. Effects like these present scenes of great beauty and hope, yet they are in reality scenes of great barrenness and desolation until the hearts of men are opened by the Spirit of God to receive the truth in the love of it. "Upon the land of My people shall come up thorns and briars; yea, upon all the houses of joy in the joyous city; because the palaces shall be forsaken; the multitude of the city shall be left; the forts and towers shall be for dens forever, a joy of wild asses, a pasture of flocks; until the Spirit be poured upon us from on high, and the wilderness be a fruitful field, and the fruitful field be counted for a forest" (Isaiah 32:13–15). No such effective and beneficial changes will take place in the moral condition of men as shall give success to the kingdom of God until this sacred influence descends, now in drops, now in more copious showers, giving fertility and gladness. Then it is that the great

Husbandman "plants in the wilderness the cedar tree, the shittah tree, and the myrtle, and the oil tree," and sets in the desert "the fir tree, and the pine, and the box tree together; that they may see, and know, and consider, and understand together, that the hand of the Lord hath done this, and the Holy One of Israel hath created it" (Isaiah 41:19–20).

A glorious day will that be when, after ages of darkness and long periods of spiritual desolation, the cheering words shall be again heard from heaven, " 'And I will no more hide My face from them; for I have poured out My Spirit upon the house of Israel,' saith the Lord God" (Ezekiel 39:29). The kingdom of Satan, that subtle and malignant spirit who dwells in the children of disobedience, and who has with so much success organized a regular system of opposition to the kingdom of God, shall be brought within narrower, and still more narrow limits, until it is ultimately subverted and overthrown. Apostate men shall be withdrawn in great numbers from their allegiance to his empire, and shall be introduced into the kingdom of God, and kept in it, and the kingdom of glory shall be hastened. We may not look for the successes of the gospel and the triumphs of truth without a divine agency. They are but instruments which we make use of, and are never effectual save when wielded by an omnipotent arm. It would be but a state of complete hopelessness to call upon men to forsake their sins, and to wait for the Son of God from heaven, without confidence in something beside an arm of flesh.

I remark then once more that there is an appropriate place for another powerful agency in advancing the kingdom of God, I mean, the power of prayer. Prayer in the closet, prayer in the domestic circle, prayer in the sanctuary, concert in prayer, everywhere, at all times and with one accord, is the great means of securing the needed influences of the Spirit, and of realizing the hopes of the Church for His coming and kingdom who is her adorable Head. Prayer touches the only spring that can possibly ensure success. By speaking, we move man; by prayer, we move God. It is through the medium of prayer that the littleness and meanness of man prevails with Omnipotence. The prayer of faith is the only power in the universe to which the great Jehovah yields. He looks upon every other power as more or less opposed to Him; but he looks upon this as a confession of man's dependence, as an appropriate homage to His greatness, and as an attraction which brings down His divine agency to the earth. The voice of prayer is a voice which God hears; it suggests reasons which He weighs; it is the expression of affections in which He delights; it is the utterance of desires which He honors, and is honored in gratifying. "If ye, being evil, know how to give good gifts to your children, how much more shall your Father which is in heaven give His Holy Spirit to them that ask Him?" (Matthew 7:11)

Men may prosper without other gifts, but they cannot prosper without God's Holy Spirit. Other gifts are for the body; this is for the soul. Other gifts are for time; this is for eternity. Earthly parents can bestow other gifts; this they cannot bestow. This is a gift purchased at a dear rate; but our heavenly Parent gives it freely, and only for the asking. Everything else may fail, but prayer has irresistible power, and that in the hour of the most dire extremity. Prayer pleads in His name, and for His sake and kingdom who bowed His heavens to dwell with and suffer for men, and whom eternally to honor is the peculiar office of the Spirit of all grace. Jesus Himself dictated the request, "Thy kingdom come!" because that kingdom, under His own condescending and gracious arrangement, needs the impulse of prayer. It solicits it now from the reader, from the writer, from men everywhere. It is now in the midst of its conflicts, and in many portions of the earth under the cloud. Its priests, its ministers are often clothed in sackcloth; its prophets prophesy in heaviness upon valleys of the slain; its subjects weep because the enemy has spread out his hand over her pleasant things. And not until more are found who cease not day or night to bow their knees before the great Hearer of prayer that the Holy Ghost may be sent down from Heaven will this dejection pass away, Zion become clothed with garments of beauty and salvation, and her hopes and expectations be measured no longer by her own resources, but His who is wonderful in working. The higher we ascend the mount of prayer, the more extended and the brighter is the prospect. A bright streak skirts the horizon, and, after long nights of ignorance and sin, the day dawns, not upon a desert and barren world, but one already watered with copious showers. The view brightens as we still ascend. It is no longer a little cloud that we see, betokening an abundance of rain, but the descending showers, the vales beneath green as the garden of the Lord.

Rivers of gladness water all the earth,
And clothe all climes with beauty.

"Thy kingdom come!" This is a great request, not merely on account of the objects it has in view, but the practical duties it involves. The spirit of prayer is the spirit of corresponding exertion; the noblest, most self-denying, and successful efforts for the coming of God's kingdom originate at the mercy seat, and find their strongest and most unwearied impulse in prayer. The suppliant who goes to the throne with this request on his lips, if he is true-hearted, possesses a strong attachment to the kingdom which the God of heaven has set up in our world, and a willingness on his part to do all in his power to promote it both in his own heart and in the hearts of his fellow-men.

There is nothing for which such a man feels so much concern as for the honor of his redeeming God and King; nothing he so fervently desires as that His character should be loved and venerated, His laws obeyed, and His claims enthroned in the hearts of those who know not God. "If I forget thee, O Jerusalem, let my right hand forget her cunning; if I do not remember thee, let my tongue cleave to the roof of my mouth; if I prefer not Jerusalem above my chief joy" (Psalm 137:5–6)! He who possesses this spirit complains not if God makes demands upon his thoughts, his time, efforts, and property, to extend this kingdom in the world; it is his privilege and honor to consecrate them. He will not offer to God that which costs him nothing. He is habitually jealous of himself, and watchful of his own heart and life, lest he should be betrayed into the inconsistency of praying for the advancement of that kingdom, for the prosperity of which he does nothing, and in which he himself has no part.

If the reader sympathizes with the writer of these pages, he has often felt rebuked and condemned by his own prayers. The achievements of prayer ought to be more in keeping with its subject and its matter. They will be so when we possess its true spirit. Would that this encouraging fact were set in its true light, and were more deeply felt by the Christian world! As certainly as effects follow their causes, in any of the visible operations of nature, "The effectual, fervent prayer of a righteous man availeth much." It is but for the spirit of the closet and the sanctuary to be more deeply felt, and uniformly acted out in the life, and the kingdom of God will come with power.

Far too weak and limited are our conceptions of the work to be done, and the agencies to be employed, in extending the kingdom of God over this lost world. Yet there is one thought I desire to impress on the mind of the reader before I close the present chapter. It is the relation which those who already belong to this kingdom bear to those who are out of it. The wicked are to be converted to God through the instrumentality of the righteous. Salvation was originally of the Jews because they were the only visible people of God. The rod of God's strength goes forth "out of Zion." So far as human instrumentality is concerned, the resources of the world are found in the Church of God. Her Scriptures and her ministry, her Sabbaths and her ordinances, her religious training of the young and her prayers, her bounty, her example, and her self-denying efforts and courage, are the hope of benighted and lost men. The Church of God constitutes a great Christian corporation for extending the boundaries and beautifying the character of God's kingdom among men. It is not for her own sake alone that she was thus incorporated, but for the sake of others, and that this divinely incorporated body of the professed children of the kingdom might take a deep and effective interest in the conversion of the world. She holds her high immunities and hopes in trust for a world that lies in wickedness.

The conscience of the Church has been slow in feeling this obligation; where it is felt and acknowledged, it has not always been responded to by a willing heart and consecrated effort. Did the Church of God now on the earth possess the self-sacrificing spirit of the churches established in the apostolic age, we might say with the apostles, "Now thanks be to God, which always causeth us to triumph in Christ, and maketh manifest the savor of His knowledge by us in every place." There has been a declension in the missionary spirit ever since the memorable age of which we are speaking. Persecution checked it, then controversy, then the corruption of prosperity and power, then a chivalrous enthusiasm, then severe persecutions, and then again the spirit of controversy, till the world extended its ascendancy, and the Church sank in almost universal apathy and indifference. The lighting up of the past fifty years has been a delightful yet faint reflection of that apostolic spirit which poured its light on Jewish and Gentile lands. It is a narrow sphere which the church occupies compared with that which she was organized to occupy, and for the occupation of which she possesses such augmented means, influences, and facilities. We want an exercised conscience in this matter; we want the love of Christ; we want the strong and healthy pulsations of glowing piety. The stream has set in; it is flowing on silently; but it must have a wider and deeper channel. Much do we need to prove the preciousness and power of the heart-searching, wrestling, effectual prayer, "Thy kingdom come!"

Where there are professions of piety, but no genuine piety at heart, there is no interest excited for the coming of God's kingdom. The spiritual welfare of men, the honor and glory of the King of Zion, have no place in the bosom of the man who lives to himself. The philanthropy that terminates in the temporal well being of men is not the noble and disinterested charity of the Bible. The charity of the Bible is stronger than the ties of humanity; it draws closer than all other ties. It attracts soul to soul. It forms a bond of attachment to those who are far off as well as those who are near. It is a sympathy which includes men of every class and climate, and will never be fully gratified until that bright day when the Son of David shall have dominion from sea to sea, and from the river to the ends of the earth.

Chapter 7

The Will of God Performed on Earth
"Thy will be done on earth as it is in heaven."

There is no higher or more absolute authority than that one being should claim the right of governing another by his own will. Yet such is the government of God. It is monarchy, absolute monarchy. He is the sole governor, and makes His will the rule of action to all creatures. His views of right and wrong, His thoughts of propriety and impropriety, are the rule. In a universe like ours, there must be a monarchy as absolute as this or there is no government at all.

God's right thus to give law is founded on His original and underived supremacy. The eternity of His existence, the supremacy of His wisdom, power, and goodness, so infinitely above those of all creatures, give Him the throne and make Him the monarch. It is a monarchy which, however unsafe in other hands, is safe in His. It is a monarchy in which all holy beings delight, and would not exchange for any other form of government. Hence we are taught to pray, "Thy will be done on earth as it is in heaven!"

There can be but one opinion as to the import of the phrase "the will of God" as it is here used. The phrase itself is taken in the Scriptures in a double sense, sometimes denoting that which shall be, and sometimes that which ought to be. The former is the will of God in His providence, or that which He has purposed; the latter is the will of God in His law, or that which He requires. This distinction should be clearly stated and understood. When the Savior says, "For whosoever shall do the will of God, the same is My brother, and My sister, and mother," the meaning of the phrase there is regarding the laws and commandments of God. So when we read of those who "do the will of God from the heart," of standing perfect and complete in all the will of God, of "living not in the lusts of men, but to the will of God," in these and similar passages the import of the phrase is the same with that just mentioned. But we find the same phrase frequently used in a different sense. Paul says, "For who hath resisted His will, who worketh all things after the counsel of His own will?" The Savior says, in view of the cross, "Not My will, but Thine be done!" And John says, "If we ask anything according to His will, He heareth us." In these last mentioned passages, the phrase signifies not the laws and commands of God, but the divine purpose or decree.

These two are very different things. The divine purpose extends to the irrational and material as well as to the rational and spiritual creation; the divine law extends only to that which is spiritual and rational. The divine purpose includes all that God means should take place; the divine law only that which He requires and forbids. The divine purpose expresses no authority and no moral obligation, and is, therefore, never a rule of action; the divine law expresses both, and is a rule of action to all to whom it is revealed. The divine purpose has respect to events, and is concerned with the consequences of human conduct, while the divine law respects the conduct of intelligent agents as such, and has nothing to do with its events and consequences.

That it is the perceptive will of God to which this prayer refers cannot admit of a question. An object obtained cannot be the object of petition. This request cannot relate to God's purpose, because His purpose is accomplished as well on the earth as it is in heaven. His counsel shall stand, and He will do all His pleasure. But it is not so with His law. His perceptive will is accounted as a strange thing; it is transgressed, abused, and vilified; and however venerated it is in higher and purer worlds, it is trampled on and despised on earth. It is this great moral code, therefore, to which this prayer refers; and the precepts and prohibitions of which we are taught to pray may be as sacredly regarded on earth as they are in heaven.

The will of God is there done in all its parts. All the obligations of the law are there fulfilled; every precept and every prohibition is regarded with reverence and love. Where God's command is known, the thing commanded, whatever it is, is done. There is no government there but the government of the divine will. All those affections of mind which are due from creatures to their Creator, from subjects to their supreme Lord, from pensioners upon the divine bounty to the first and the greatest of all givers, and from redeemed sinners to their all-sufficient and gracious Redeemer, are there enkindled and sustained. All that is elevating in complacency and confidence in the divine character, all that is amiable and lovely in that lowliness and sweetness of mind that are the fruits of the divine Spirit, all that is peaceful in resignation, joyous in gratitude, and adoring in praise, is there mingled and blended in the beauties of holiness.

There are no rival deities there, and no idolatry to subvert the throne of the Most High. There is no profanity or irreverence, but every expression of filial fear. There is no violation of the Sabbath; that glorious world is one vast temple, and its revolving ages one everlasting day of holy rest. There is no form, or modification of holy affection toward God which does not there exist, and is not acted out.

Nor are there any violations there of the great law of love to fellow intelligences. There are no infringements upon the claims of social piety, no mutual relations inverted, no ties torn asunder, no principles of subordination destroyed, no envious or cold, unfeeling heart. There is no murderous hand or malignant intention, no furious and revengeful passion, no harshness or cruelty, no unkindness, or even inattention and negligence. There are no revolting scenes of impurity, no haunts of licentiousness, and no lascivious eye. There are no locks, nor bars, nor prisons, nor courts of justice, nor pilfering, nor plunder, nor any species or suspicion of fraud. There is no lying tongue or covetous desire. Truth, that strong bond of society, that firm foundation of confidence and intercourse, remains inviolate, while all those inordinate desires after earthly objects and enjoyments, which so disturb the tranquility and repose of earth, are subdued and extinguished by the charity that "seeketh not her own." Heaven presents the purest, noblest, loveliest character because it is implicitly subject to the will of God. It asks for no reason of its conduct but God's will. And therefore its obedience is perfect in all its departments. It has no blemishes, no cloud in its hemisphere, no shadow in its horizon, no spot on its disk, no waxing and waning light, but a steady, pure, and full-orbed splendor.

The will of God is there obeyed also by all its inhabitants. In that immense family, there are diversities of rank, different orders of intelligence, and various measures of moral rectitude, as "one star differeth from another star in glory." There are the angels who never fell, with all their different degrees of excellence. There are the unnumbered millions redeemed from among men, from all the climes and languages of earth, from the little infant to the tried piety of hoary years, and from the thief on the cross to the aged and martyred Paul. But with all this varied extent and degree of excellence, and all this differing splendor, the same spirit pervades the whole; all possess the same elements of excellence. There is no jar in their society and no discord in their song. Within the vast compass of this immense population, throughout all these unexplored regions, amid the whole of this vast assemblage of existences, from the highest to the lowest, there is not a bosom that does not glow with holy ardor to do the will of God. One sinning mind would poison these sources of joy. There is no lawless planet there, no unsubjugated province, no land of darkness, no pagan island, no habitation of cruelty, not a dwelling of wickedness, nor even a revolting heart.

In heaven, the will of God is also done with sincerity and cheerfulness. There is no hypocrisy there; no formal sacrifice is offered on that altar. The outward conduct is there governed by first governing the willing and warm affections. Obedience is not a yoke at which pure and sinless spirits strain, but is in every view a pleasant, agreeable, delightful service. There is no pensiveness, no depression, no gloom in that blessed society, but all that is buoyant and cheerful. It is not the abstract sense of duty, the heavy bond of obligation, the solemn and fearful sanction of law, and the cold and cheerless impression of necessity merely that constrains their acquiescence. It is the sweeter, stronger cord of love, irresistibly fascinating them with its charms, and drawing their willing, gratified minds as with the bands of a man. In this low world, true religion is an exotic, an unnatural and unindigenous plant, confined and stinted in its growth, and sometimes a meager, dwarfish, and ungainly thing. It partakes of the cold soil and cheerlessness of this low earth, never arriving at maturity, and sometimes blooms just to fade. But what pencil can paint, or what poetry describe, its beauty and fragrance when transplanted to the skies? No longer some depressed and drooping floweret, it is like Sharon's rose, unfolding its leaves on its native bed. No longer weak and sickly, it is like a vigorous, healthy scion from the Tree of Life, fair and luxuriant, fragrant with blossoms, and yielding its fruit every month. It is the joy (I almost said it is the mirth) of heaven to obey the statutes of its King. Obedience is an employment which nourishes, and draws toward it all their ardor and sensibility. The perception, the reason, the judgment, and the memory are all joyfully employed in such a service. Even the imagination, that ungoverned and wandering faculty which here on earth is so often the sport of temptation, and the plaything of the arch-deceiver, there exerts its magic and hallowed influence, ever supplying the materials of some new service, some new purpose of devotion, some new scene of still more gratified holiness and exquisite joy. There obedience is indeed the obedience of thought and deliberate purpose; but it is also the obedience of love. It has the wings of emotion and desire. Love is the element in which pure spirits breathe. Love is the soul of heaven, strong and urgent, swift to do His will, hearkening to the voice of His Word.

In heaven, the will of God is likewise done perfectly and forever. Its holy inhabitants are like Him because they see Him as He is. Everything there is so full of God; creation, providence, and redemption are there displaying forth such perpetual exhibitions of the divine nature that they cannot but be discerned and enjoyed; and because they are discerned and enjoyed, they transform the soul into their own likeness. The flow of holy affections is there constant and resistless, and "clear as crystal"; and their strength and vigor remain forever unabated. There are no seasons of languor and declension, and no apostasy and backsliding. No wandering thought, no vain desire, no unperfected emotion there creeps into the soul. There is no backwardness nor unfruitfulness, but all the activity and fervor which the soul is capable of exercising. There is no weariness nor satiety. Ten thousand times ten thousand, and thousands of thousands, cease not day nor night from their active service or their anthems of praise. There the soul eagerly cleaves to, affectionately admires, and constantly rests on God. Its thoughts and desires are concentrated in this single object, pleased and satisfied with God as its portion, acting from Him as its Author, for Him as its Master, and to Him as its End. Eternity rolls on, and He who is holy is holy still.

Thus is the will of God done in heaven in all its parts by every individual, sincerely and cheerfully, perfectly and forever. And is there not a reason for the prayer that it should be thus done on earth? For this Christ has taught His disciples, in every age of the world, to pray, "Thy will be done on earth as it is in heaven." Why ought we to pray thus? Let us give an answer to this inquiry.

It is not out of place to submit the remark that the law of God is no less binding on the earth than it is in heaven. Its obligations are real throughout the whole range of God's dominions. Wherever intelligent beings exist, they are bound by it. If angels are bound by it, so are men; and if one world of intelligent agents is bound by it, so are all worlds. There is no more excuse for violating it on earth than for violating it in heaven. Nothing can dissolve, suspend, or at all impair the obligations of men to do the will of God as universally, sincerely, fully, and perfectly as it is done in heaven. As it alters not the nature of transgression that it is committed in secret or in the light of day, at home or abroad, in the eastern or western hemisphere of this terraqueous globe; so it alters not its nature that it were committed in the terrestrial rather than the celestial sphere. The binding force of the divine law depends on the nature of the Lawgiver, and on the relations which exist between Him and His subjects; and not until these are destroyed or altered can there be any change in the law. This is the only true doctrine of moral obligation. The will of the superior binds the inferior everywhere. And we have much reason to pray that this rebellious world may recognize, both in theory and in practice, the principle that there is no virtue but in obedience to the will of God.

But this is not all. While every man should obey the law of God merely because it is law and an expression of His will, it is a right rule to which he is subject. It is as reasonable that the will of God be done on earth as that it should be done in heaven. Though its reasonableness does not augment our obligations to obedience, yet is it one of the motives for it. All the considerations which show the reasonableness of doing God's will in heaven also show that it is reasonable it should be done on earth. Wickedness is unreasonable, always and everywhere; nor is there anything so reasonable, so beautiful, so lovely in the universe as obedience to God. Whatever is right, the will of God requires; it forbids nothing but wickedness. It is impossible that too much rectitude be required of any order of intelligences, nor can they be governed by a law that is too holy. The inhabitants of earth are no more dependent for holiness than the inhabitants of heaven; and if they were, we have not now to learn that the dependence of men does not render it less reasonable that they should do what is right. Why is it not reasonable that the will of God should be done on earth as it is in heaven? Is it reasonable for those immortal princes to obey their Sovereign, and is it unreasonable for man? Shall those bright partakers of the divine glory, those favored attendants at the heavenly court, consent to the law that is good? And shall men, abject and fallen, contend with their Maker and complain that His ways are not equal?

Obedience to God's will would produce a high degree of happiness in the earth as well as in heaven. The foundation on which the happiness of thinking beings rests is their obedience to the divine will. Individually and relatively, as parts and as a whole, this earth would be supremely happy if it possessed the character of heaven. We know the happy effects even of the very imperfect holiness which good men possess in the present life. Where that moral transformation which results in the sinless purity of the heavenly world is but begun, what new affections and hopes, what divine peace and joy, are imparted to the soul! When first the heart is dissolved with the mild influences of the Spirit of grace, and imbued with the love of God and man, what sweet repose possesses it! Its struggles, for a while, seem to be over; the alarms of conscience are still. And not until the workings of iniquity revive are this tranquility and joy disturbed. And when in his progressive career of sanctification the regenerated man becomes more holy, and the power of indwelling corruption is broken and prostrate, how does His light break forth as the morning, and His joys become like the spring tide when it overflows its banks! Witness the blessedness of David and Paul, and others in later days, when their transported spirits could not utter their ecstasy because they were clogged and fettered in this prison-house of clay. Even this were a prelibation of heaven. Extended over all the habitations of men, it would make this earth an exquisitely happy world. How pure and transporting the joy if, instead of this, the will of God were obeyed on earth as it is in heaven! Over all the regions of the globe every pulse would beat, every heart throb, and every tongue respond to the claims of holy love. Disorder and tumult would be unknown, the oppressor's rod would be broken, and injustice and war would no more ravage the habitations of men. Individual quietude and social joy would change the face of every land, and nothing would be seen but spectacles of loveliness and beauty, while everywhere would be heard the voice of thanksgiving and praise. How serene and clear the light that would then be diffused over the creation! What a picture of the bosom of angels! Like what a sea of glass would the minds of men become, everywhere placid and unruffled, and without a ripple on its surface! What a world will this be when God shall thus create Jerusalem a-rejoicing, and make her people a joy! And when, compared with this new spiritual creation, the first heavens and earth shall not be remembered, nor come into mind!

Still further, God would be as truly honored and glorified by the obedience of earth as He is by the obedience of heaven. He is eminently exalted by the sinless perfection of the heavenly world. Every tongue there speaks well of God; every mind sees Him as He is; every object reflects His glory; every heart loves and exalts Him; and the only emulation is to ascribe the highest honors to His name. There is no other way of honoring and exalting God but by doing His will. When the same spirit glows in the bosom of men as in the bosom of angels, the same honors will be paid Him from the altars of this world that now ascend from the heavenly sanctuary. Anticipate this delightful spectacle. Behold these creatures of God, in all their varieties of habitation and name, and in all the gradations of their intellectual endowment, never varying from the standard of rectitude; failing in no precept, unceasingly devoted to their duty and from the best spirit, chargeable with nothing that can be condemned or reproached, all doing the will of God as it is done in heaven; and what a field of light, what a sea of glory were presented by such a renovated creation! No longer would His name be dishonored, who calls Himself "our Father who art in heaven"; no longer would His government be defamed, His designs impeached and opposed, and His honors taken from Him. But everywhere He would be acknowledged as God over all, blessed forever. Princes and subjects, young men and maidens, old men and children, would give Him the honor which is His due. His name would be great among the heathen, and, in every place, incense and a pure offering would be offered on His altar.

Nor is this all. In some respects, God is even more honored by the obedience of earth than by the obedience of heaven. The planet on which we dwell is a peculiar world. It has properties and relations altogether peculiar to itself. There are no such expressions of the divine goodness made to any other world as are made to this one. Nowhere does it assume the form of favor to the guilty except to men. Nowhere else does it flow through the channel of a Savior's blood; and nowhere else does it cost so many efforts of wisdom and power throughout all the dispensations of a widely extended providence. When men on the earth become holy, they are a peculiar people, and show forth the praises of Him who hath brought them "out of darkness into His marvelous light." They differ from all other beings in the universe. They sustain a relation to the once atoning and now reigning Savior, which other beings and other worlds do not sustain. Others have gained the heavenly inheritance by their own righteousness; inhabitants of earth are the purchase of the Savior's blood, and the reward of His obedience unto death. Others have been created and preserved; these have been redeemed and sanctified. Others are beautiful in themselves; these are beautiful through the comeliness which He put upon them, and on that account have moral perceptions, emotions, and joys to which others are strangers, and a song in which others can never unite. God is glorified by the obedience of the unfallen, but their love and admiration flow forth in none of the forms peculiar to redeemed sinners. We are told that "there is joy in heaven over one sinner that repenteth more than over ninety and nine just persons who need no repentance." And who does not see that when such a population becomes holy, such rebels become children, such outcasts heirs of God, there is glory to God in the highest degree? When it is seen and known to principalities and powers in heavenly places that, in defiance of the machinations of the prince of darkness and the invincible depravity of man, the kingdom of Christ and the empire of mercy are triumphant, what honors will be recovered to the Great Supreme? In what unequalled beauty will the reflected excellence of His nature cover the earth as the waters cover the sea, and how will holy ones look down from heaven to say, "The whole earth is full of His glory!" How will the mountains echo it to the valleys, and the valleys roll it back again to the mountains, that "the Lord God omnipotent reigneth!" How will continent proclaim it to continent, and ocean waft it to the main, that "the kingdoms of this world are become the kingdoms of our Lord and His Christ!" And what ascriptions of honor, what thunderings of praise, in one mighty concert of the fallen with the unfallen, like the sound of many waters, will pour forth their sublime and unceasing Allelujahs to God and the Lamb!

Such is the import, and such are some of the reasons for the petition urged in the text. In view of the preceding thoughts, who may not with strong propriety lay his hand upon his mouth? The present condition of the Church and world is mournfully affecting to every Christian mind (I say of the Church as well as the world because, even in her fairest and holiest portions, the will of God is so imperfectly done). When we consider how much more holy the people of God might become, how much more happy and exalted, how much more conspicuous the spiritual kingdom of God might be among the nations, and how much more subservient to the glory of its great Prince and Savior, we feel condemned before God and man.

If from the Church we look at the world, our eye affects our heart. It is a world fallen by its iniquity, and under the wrath and curse of God. Oh, how vile, how abject it is! How dishonored! What indifference to God, what practical atheism, what subversion of religion and moral order, what sottish ignorance, what depraved passions and shocking immoralities disfigure the aspect and mar the form of human society! And when we look beyond the pale of Christian lands, what do we see but men sunk still deeper in pollution and sin, prostrated in wretchedness, corrupted and loathsome, and covered with the pall of sin and death?

Can this be the world where men have been taught to pray, "Thy will be done on earth, as it is done in heaven"? How desolate! How bewildered! What gloom and terror! "Darkness covers the earth, and gross darkness the people" (Isaiah 60:2). Three-fourths of the world in which we dwell do not as yet know that they may call God their Father, and approach His throne in the new and living way. Not a ray of light from the cross has ever descended on their path. Over what vast regions does the prince of darkness extend his dominion! With the exception of a few bright spots, or, at best, a few narrow zones, this dark and iron-hearted empire enwraps the globe. Alas, that such a picture should ever be realized in the world where the Savior died, and where He has left on record such a prayer!

Yet, notwithstanding this, this very prayer suggests a ground of hope. The Savior would not have instructed His disciples to pray, as He has here instructed them, had He not designed to bring men extensively to the knowledge and obedience of His truth. He has predicted that "all the ends of the earth shall remember, and turn unto the Lord, and all the kindreds of the nations shall worship before Him" (Psalm 22:27). Dark as is the prospect, therefore; the rays which already, like the pale twilight of the morning, pierce the gloom are destined to shine more and more unto the perfect day. He who has taught us this prayer is "God manifest in the flesh." He is the Author of that gospel which is the wisdom of God and the power of God to salvation, and whose mighty agency, like the Spirit of God moving upon the face of the waters, is destined to give form, order, and beauty to this moral chaos and create all things anew.

Yes, there is hope for the recovery of this apostate world. Our Immanuel is on the throne, and His heart of love is bound up in this glorious consummation. From the top of Calvary, these clouds that settle upon the earth are seen passing away. Just as certainly as Jesus died and rose again, "the glory of the Lord shall be revealed, and all flesh shall see it together." Whose heart shall not be inspirited with this confidence? To secure this predicted end, God gave His Son to die, sends His Spirit to dwell with men; reveals His Word, and lays on His Church the responsibility of sending His gospel to every creature. I blush to ask how little we have done that the will of God might be performed on earth as it is in heaven. How little have we suffered, and in how few respects have we denied ourselves so that these designs of Heaven's mercy may be accomplished!

Who, then, will not make frequent use of this great petition? Whether we look to pagan or to Christian lands, in what tones of solicitude may these blood-bought churches hear the cry, "Pray for us; pray for us!" And who will not respond, "Thy kingdom come, Thy will be done, on earth as it is in heaven"? There wanders some poor pagan, who never heard a sermon, nor saw a Bible, and who knows not that the blood of Jesus Christ cleanses from all sin. He is intelligent and thoughtful, but he is the victim of a dark and dreadful idolatry. His mind is merged in the shades of impenetrable night. Over his prospects for eternity are collected heavy and dense clouds of unappeased indignation. And even here, where we ourselves dwell, what darkness covers large portions of the land! Cities, villages, colleges, schools, families, the rich and the poor, old and young, in almost untold numbers, are strangers to the hopes of the gospel. Some of them are thoughtless, and some of them are anxious, struggling for the assurance of a happy immortality. We do not count them, either in pagan or Christian lands, by hundreds or by thousands, but by millions! Millions are living without God, and are soon to die without hope!

Approach and see them one by one as they drop into eternity. It is a melancholy chamber and a dark hour. That face is pale. That eye is dim with tears. That bosom is torn with anguish. Those lips quiver with agony, and the despondent sufferer draws his last breath in despair! One by one, these millions are sinking into such a death. Yet, through our mercy, they might obtain mercy; immortal as they are, they may gain a happy immortality.

Oh, for more of the spirit of this precious prayer! The Savior would have His people utter it every day that they live. His Word goes forth in vain without the prayer for His accompanying grace. The most disheartening, the most overwhelming obstacles oppose it at every step. It is not in Paul, nor Apollos; it is not in ministers, nor means to arouse the lethargy or disturb the deeply embedded depravity of the human earth. If men are ever led to do God's will, those who have an interest at the throne of grace must be often on their knees. They must stretch out their hands unto God. They must lie on their faces at His feet. With hope and confidence (and not unfrequently with strong crying and many tears), they must carry the souls of men to His throne. We cannot hope too much from Him. We shall enjoy for ourselves copious showers of divine grace as soon as the spirit of supplication is copiously poured upon us from on high. The world will enjoy them as soon as the churches have more of the spirit of prayer. When we come nearest the throne, then let us remember this precious request. If ever we lean on Jesus' bosom, and feel that we have intercourse with Him; if ever we enjoy seasons of enlargement in prayer, and have the sweet consciousness that we are allowed to have power with God, let us fill our mouth with arguments, and plead fervently and importunately that His will may be done on earth as it is in heaven.

Chapter 8

Dependence for Temporal Blessings
"Give us this day our daily bread."

When the Great Teacher undertakes to sum up, in seven short sentences, the whole matter of the sinner's prayer, we are to expect that every one of them is of great importance. If wise and good men, or even holy angels, had had the form of this prayer, while they would not have overlooked temporal blessings, it is not probable they would have given so prominent a place to the request, "Give us this day our daily bread." We cannot too often call to mind that all the dispensations of God are consistent with one another. Although He has made man a creature destined for immortality, He has made him to partake of blessings that are mortal. He must have food and raiment, with numberless other attendant mercies, in order rightly to pursue the great ends of his immortality. "Your heavenly Father knoweth that ye have need of all these things." It is because He has connected the highest principle of happiness with the lowest gradation of that happiness that in this summary of petitions the Lord Jesus has put so high an estimate on the good things of the present world. True religion neither idolizes nor overlooks these things. It gives them their proper place; and while it reproves and condemns the avarice and sensuality of a worldly mind, it at the same time rebukes the stiff severity, the studied abstemiousness, the professed indifference to worldly good, which are equally at war with the promptings of our nature, and the claims of duty to God, to ourselves, and to our fellow-men. Our object is to present some expansion of this request, and to select and enforce the great principles it contains. I will give four of them here:

1. For the supply of their temporal wants, men are dependent on God. Prayer is a distinct recognition of dependence. When the Savior puts the petition into our mouths, "Give us this day our daily bread," He not only teaches the abstract doctrine of our dependence, but that we should be in the habit of acknowledging it. Just in the proportion in which men lose sight of this thought, or live in the neglect of this duty, are they sinking into blank atheism. Temporal enjoyments are no more the result of chance and contingency than the beautiful and wondrous world in which we dwell. Natural causes may be the means and instruments of their production, but they are not the authors of them. They form no constituent part either of the firmament above us or of the earth beneath us; nor are any of the numerous physical combinations which give form and substance to them under the control either of angels or men. The industry of man may be employed in procuring them, but his very toils furnish affecting admonitions of his dependence.

We are prone to stop at second causes in our survey of the entire range of temporal good; but the spirit of genuine piety stops not short of the great First Cause. Not all the second causes in the universe ever gave fertility to the harvest field, clothed the silk worm, or called into being the humblest flower. "Beware," said God to His ancient people, "lest when thy herds and thy flocks multiply, and thy silver and thy gold is multiplied, and all that thou hast is multiplied; lest thy heart be lifted up, and thou forget the Lord thy God, and thou say in thine heart, 'My power, and the might of my hand hath gotten me this wealth.' " This would be neither sound philosophy nor true religion. "The eyes of all wait upon Thee, and Thou givest them their meat in due season" (Psalm 145:15). The providence of God interweaves and mingles itself with all the affairs and circumstances of men. It extends itself alike to the drop of a bucket and to the ocean, to the small dust of the balance and to the whole material universe, to every individual of the human family and to the entire race. The goodness that visits the greater also visits the less. If the meanest of the human family were too insignificant to be noticed, he would be too insignificant to be heard, and would be alike absolved from the duty and debarred from the privilege of prayer. The children of poverty and want may have deeper impressions of their dependence than the sons and daughters of opulence; while in sober verity the imperial purple, the splendid palace, and the sumptuous fare of princes are as truly from God as the coarse garb, the shattered tenement, and the scanty fare of the beggar in his rags. The latter may be more ready to disclaim all reliance on other sources because their daily bread must be dealt out to them, and they must beg it at God's hand. But the rich are not less dependent on the same almighty Parent. Their abundant resources, their wide domains, their splendid edifices, their costly equipage, and their gold and credit, are all in His hands who gives and takes away when and where He pleases. It is not necessary for Him to work a miracle in order to disappoint the expectations of the most confident, defeat their proudest hopes, and overturn the loftiest edifice their pride has reared.

Nature herself teaches us that our insufficiency is absolute while God's sufficiency is boundless. How many secondary causes—not one of which is under any human control—must be preserved in successful operation in order to secure His daily subsistence to a single individual of the human family! What a delicate and nice adjustment of all the laws of nature must be preserved in order to furnish a person food to eat and raiment to put on! What a multitude of bodies in the planetary system must be constantly and wisely directed in order to shelter him from the summer's heat and the winter's cold! What masses of matter must be arranged and propelled; what orbs must shine and what clouds obscure; what vapors must be arrested in mid-air or gently distil their moisture; what springs must be filled and what rivers must flow; what tempests must agitate and what zephyrs must breathe; what unnumbered processes in the vast laboratory of the universe must all be preserved in their due and fitting action, and how many intelligent agents sustained in their course of plodding industry, in order to furnish those blessings which make human life cheerful and happy! Nay, all this is needful even to furnish the wardrobe of the most humble cottager, or to procure a cup of cold water, a loaf of bread, or one poor barleycorn. Had we an angel's eye and wing to follow out and trace the ten thousand influences of that great First Cause, and mark His unwearied care and offices of love, how should we discern His almighty and all-pervading providence, and how deeply should we feel that in His hand is the soul of every living thing!

To instructions like these, we may also add the lessons of personal experience. You began the world poor; and God has not only taken care of you, but given you unexpected prosperity. Every shower and every drought, every storm and every calm, every revolution in human affairs at home and abroad, every year, and it may be every day, while fraught with calamity to others, has only served to heap up riches to yourselves. Or it may be that it has been your lot to experience sad and melancholy reverses. Your resources have failed; your riches have taken to themselves wings and passed away; your industry and contrivance have all been in vain; calamity after calamity has invaded your comforts, and everything has seemed to be against you. And is there no overruling Providence in these things? Is there no dependence of the creature upon the

Creator? "Who knoweth not, in all these, that the hand of the Lord hath wrought this" (Job 12:9)? What we ourselves seem to procure is from Him; what we receive from others is from Him; what comes to us we know not whence, we know not how, is from Him. What, in the view of man, is most contingent is designed by Him. His providence is daily employed in this wonderful provision. Our dependence is as absolute and unceasing as His superintending care and bounty.

2. *What is thus supplied to the children of men is, to them, a mere gratuity.* From men we can often claim temporal good; it is ours by contract, and for services rendered; we have a right to it by the decision of law, and can enforce that right by legal process. But we have no such claim on God. He owes us nothing. We may use the language of suppliants, "Give us this day our daily bread," but we have no claim of merit or of right. It is all of His mercy, and not of our own deserving. Man's dependence renders his daily bread God's gift. It belongs to God, and our lives themselves are His. Gabriel himself cannot say of the smallest and most obscure gem that adorns his crown that it is of his own procuring. For who has first "given to the Lord, and it shall be recompensed to him again; for of Him, and to Him, and through Him, are all things" (Romans 11:36). He is not indebted to the holiest of them, nor may one among them all, either among the fallen or unfallen, take from a thread to a shoe latchet unless he first asks it of God. Earthly good becomes ours only as we ask and God gives it. The most laborious may not touch the fruits of the ground he has cultivated, and which he has gathered and garnered, without first asking leave of his heavenly Father. God requires us to ask; it is promised only to those who ask. We have the prospect of God's blessing with our daily mercies only as we ask for them. They become a curse rather than a blessing when we take them without asking. To those who will not lay it to

heart to give glory unto His name, God says, "I will curse your blessings; yea, I have cursed them already; because ye do not lay it to heart." When the haughty king of Babylon pillaged the vessels of gold and silver from the Temple at Jerusalem, He who dwelleth not in temples made with hands held him responsible for the sacrilege. And He would have men know that this rich and beautiful earth is His temple; that these unfathomed stores of wealth gathered from its recesses, or harvested from its surface, all belong to Him, and that, when bestowed, they are a mere gratuity, given freely, and without any remuneration to their Author. The rich and great have as little to give for them as the most humble poor. They themselves are nothing; they have nothing; they can do nothing and enjoy nothing without Him.

And if man's dependence renders his daily bread God's gift, much more does his sinfulness render it so. As a sinner, he has no right to divine blessings of any kind. As to the creature's right to claim anything from the Creator, it is simply this: so long as he remains innocent, he has a claim upon Him for protection. It would be wrong not to exempt him from punishment, because he does not deserve punishment. But when man by sin forfeited his life, the greater blessing, his claim to every smaller blessing was forfeited also. Had there been no forfeiture, there had been no such thing as suffering for want of the necessaries of life; and this is one form in which God has written this forfeiture on man's actual condition.

Fallen, sinful, and sinning man; man who not only owes God all that he is and has, but who has forfeited all by his transgressions; man who has become so deeply indebted to the divine justice that, but for the timely interposition of sovereign mercy, nothing had awaited him but the worm and the flames, may well understand that, so far from having any claims on God, whatever he receives that is better than the equitable recompense of his iniquity is gift, is bounty, is the "gift of God through Jesus Christ."

It is not a thought to which the minds of Christian men are strangers that their daily bread is conveyed to them in channels opened at the cross. This otherwise barren and desert earth has become fertile, its clouds surcharged with blessings, and its revolving seasons, and the patient toil of its inhabitants, have become fruitful in mercies only through the mediation of that Great Sufferer who arrested the sentence that would otherwise have consigned it to destruction. God might withhold their daily bread, and treat them better than their deservings. And when bestowed, it is without any equivalent or compensation. It is a daily present; it is a donation from Him whose eye never slumbers and whose goodness is never weary.

Many a man who disclaims all right to the bounties of God's providence in theory has a false and secret sense of his worthiness of temporal good. We should be disabused of this ensnaring thought, if we would rightly ask for our daily bread. It diminishes our impressions of the divine bounty, and weakens our sense of grateful obligation. If we are made to differ from others, it is God who makes us to differ. God is everything to us, but what are we to Him? If it is a proof of an ungenerous and dishonorable mind to be indifferent to the accepted bounty of men, and human liberality becomes a thankless and irksome service, where it is imperiously claimed rather than gratefully acknowledged, still more ungenerous and dishonorable is it to complain that heaven's bounty is scantily or grudgingly bestowed, or when bestowed liberally, that it is no more than we had a right to expect. It contributes not a little to our enjoyment of God's goodness to dwell upon it as His gift, and to think of Him as the greatest of givers. To know and feel this, to feel it when we pray, is the cheered and grateful sentiment of true piety, the blessedness of angels, and the joy of heaven.

3. This request inculcates an implicit reliance on divine goodness and bounty for all that we need. It is a great privilege to trust with undisturbed tranquility on the bountiful providence of our Father who is in heaven. He has encouraged us to do this by the very privilege of prayer. "In all thy ways acknowledge God; so shall thy barns be filled with plenty, and thy presses burst out with new wine" (Proverbs 3:10). "What man is there of you that is a father, who if his son ask of him bread, will he give him a stone? or if he ask a fish, will he give him a serpent? or if he ask an egg, will he give him a scorpion? If ye then, being evil, know how to give good gifts to your children, how much more shall your Father which is in heaven give good things to them that ask him" (Matthew 7:9–12).

Nothing can be more touching than such an appeal as this. We are needy; we are unworthy; infants are not more dependent; yet may we spread our wants before Him as a child before a Father. "The young lions do lack, and suffer hunger; but they that seek the Lord shall not want any good thing" (Psalm 34:10). He gives His children things present as well as things to come. He assures the poorest of them all that bread shall be given him, and his waters shall be sure. There is no other to whom we may with entire confidence commit all our temporal concerns, casting all our care upon Him because He careth for us. He will not trifle with our wants, nor turn away our prayer, nor His mercy from us. He who fed Israel in the desert and Elijah at the brook, He who decks the lily and beautifies the rose, will much more clothe those even of little faith. "Behold the fowls of the air; for they sow not, neither do they reap, nor gather into barns; yet your heavenly Father feedeth them; are ye not much better than they" (Matthew 6:26)? The life is more than meat, and the body than raiment! Life He has already given; and He who bestowed the greater will not withhold the lesser. He who first gave these mortal and perishing bodies, and breathed into them the breath of life, unsolicited and before they were asked for, will not, unless we trifle with the laws of His providence, and sinfully neglect the appointed means, deny that which is necessary to preserve the life He gave. Nay, we have stronger grounds for confidence. "He who spared not His own Son, but delivered Him up for us all, how shall He not with Him also freely give us all things" (Romans 8:32)? After such a demonstration of His goodness, who will question His readiness to supply minor wants, now that there is a free and unimpeded channel opened by which the divine goodness may flow to the guilty?

There is not only no reasonable desire for the gratification of which the means are not provided, but the God of providence looks beyond the circle of actual want, and is sumptuous in His provision for the comfort of men, for their convenience, and even for their luxury. "Marvelous are Thy works, Lord God Almighty, and that my soul knoweth right well! How precious are Thy thoughts unto me, O God; how great is the sum of them! If I should count them, they are more in number than the sand" (Psalm 139:17–18). There is a richness, a munificence and constancy in God's goodness which rebukes distrust. Long, very long has it been continued, without any intermission, to this rebellious and ungrateful world, extending itself from year to year, from century to century, from age to age. It never slumbers and never sleeps; it never relapses into a state of insensibility, or forgetfulness.

We distrust the bounty of creatures. One of the deepest trials to which humanity is subjected is to be dependent on creatures. Men feel the bitterness in the uncertainty of this dependence not only because it is humbling to their pride, but because it defeats their expectations. But the divine bounty needs not be distrusted; it is never bestowed capriciously, because it takes its rise from unfailing, overflowing sources; its sources are neither sealed up by the demerits of its objects nor exhausted by their poverty. Disquietude and distrust, therefore, are out of place in creatures who have access to God. Perplexing uneasiness, carking cares, and corroding solicitude are worse than useless because they render us the less fit to ask, to receive, to labor, and to enjoy. They are at war with piety, with the reliance the Bible warrants, and the confidence that God will not disappoint. The fault will be our own if He does not give us our daily bread, and if we do not live securely under His care; if His sun does not shine upon us all the day, and His dew lies all night upon our branch; if we sing not with the sweet Psalmist of Israel, "I will both lay me down in peace and sleep, for Thou, Lord, only makest me dwell in safety" (Psalm 4:8). Men who profess to trust in the promise of God for their eternal salvation are often slow of heart to trust Him for the things of time. It would be well that they bring their faith to this practical test. They give themselves credit for more faith than they have who cannot trust Him for temporal favors.

4. Our desires for temporal good should be moderate. "Give us this day our daily bread." This prayer regulates the amount of our wants and the measure of our desires. They are limited to a competency. If God's will so decides our destiny ("having food and raiment"), we should "learn therewith to be content." We should be willing to live from day to day, fed by God, and from His table. Where our own duty is faithfully performed, we may not be anxious for tomorrow's bread; God would have us ever coming to Him. We are not sure of tomorrow; we may not need His bounty then; for "What is your life? It is even a vapor that appeareth for a little while, and then vanisheth away" (James 4:14). Time flies, and the stream of life is ebbing away. That distant, uncertain thing, tomorrow, would have crowned the most ardent hopes but for the grave. When it came, it brought only a cypress wreath. While we covet the good things of this world, the almond tree flourishes on our head, the shroud is weaving for us, and the dark and narrow house becomes our home. Whatever other Scriptures may justify a prudent forethought for the things of this world, the petition which we are amplifying obviously gives no countenance to the spirit of hoarding up. If a Christian man were to make the experiment, he would find it a very difficult thing to pray for great wealth. The spirit of covetousness and the spirit of prayer do not dwell together in the same bosom. We are instructed to ask only as we need; there is danger in asking more. God may give more, but it is not safe to ask for more lest He should say of us, as He did of His restive and grasping people of other days, "I gave them their request, but sent leanness into their souls."

It is a beautiful remark of Lord Bacon, bad as he was, "Seek not proud wealth; but such as thou mayest get justly, use soberly, distribute cheerfully, and leave contentedly." Wealth is desirable not for its own sake, but merely for the wants it supplies. In itself, it is an abstract, imaginary thing; and where it is possessed it frequently creates more wants than it gratifies. It is desirable, mainly, to augment influence and extend the facilities of doing good. That accomplished statesman and jurist, the late William Wirt, a name that will be long illustrious and venerated in American history, on this topic makes the following touching observations: "Excessive wealth is neither glory nor happiness. The cold and sordid wretch who thinks only of himself; who draws his head within his shell, and never puts it out, but for the purpose of lucre and ostentation; who looks upon his fellow-creatures, not only without sympathy, but with arrogance and insolence, as if they were made to be his vassals, and he to be their lord; as if they were made for no other purpose than to pamper his avarice, or to contribute to his aggrandizement; such a man may be rich, but, trust me, he never can be happy, nor virtuous, nor great. There is in a fortune a golden mean, which is the appropriate region of virtue and intelligence. Be content with that; and if the horn of plenty overflow, let its droppings fall upon your fellow men; let them fall like the droppings of honey in the wilderness, to cheer the faint and weary pilgrim."

It is a sad thought that wealth is essential to distinction. It is not so. The voice of conscience, the voice of reason, the voice of God, announces it is not so. Wealth alone is not worth living for. Do not sigh for wealth. Do not envy the splendor and ease of the affluent. The most wealthy are often the most in want. "A man's life consisteth not in the abundance of the things which he possesseth" (Luke 12:15). Where wealth is the most eagerly sought after, it is the least satisfying. No wise man will ever venture to pray that he might be rich. Let a man be thankful if, by exemplary diligence, he can procure a comfortable living; if with this he can be cheerful and happy, he has the earnest of more, and, what is of much greater consequence, he has the pledge that ore will not be his ruin. An eminent merchant of this metropolis, distinguished no less for his liberality than his integrity and success in business, and who was a most exemplary ruling elder in one of the churches, remarked to this writer many years ago, "Sir, God has been pleased to give me a large share of this world's goods; but I have never dared to ask for more than my daily bread."

It is no common attainment rightly to regulate our desires for temporal blessings. There is nothing I regard to which a good man may be more easily beguiled and blinded, or in which he may trust his own heart less. All our desires and requests for temporal mercies should be constantly and implicitly referred to the will of God. He only knows what is best to give, and He only is able and willing to dispense His bounty in that measure which is dictated by unerring wisdom. This should satisfy us. Not to be satisfied with this is to have the heart of a rebel.

Our desires for this world should also all be regulated by desires still more earnest for spiritual blessings. This is the great object for which we should live and labor: "Seek ye first the kingdom of God, and His righteousness." "Whether ye eat or drink, or whatsoever ye so, do all to the glory of God." We ought to be deeply anxious, and the prayer should often be on our lips, that we may not be among those to whom God gives all their portion in this life. Better a thousand fold to live and die like Lazarus than like Dives, and hear the affecting admonition at the last, "Son, remember that thou in thy lifetime receivedst thy good things." It was the prayer of Agur, "Give me neither poverty nor riches; feed me with food convenient for me, lest I be full, and deny Thee, and say, 'Who is the Lord?' Or lest I be poor, and steal, and take the name of God in vain." Abject poverty may be best for us; when it is so, God will send it; when He sends it, it becomes us to submit to His providence without repining; and when we are this submissive, He will give grace to preserve us from its snares.

Still less can the human heart be trusted with overgrown riches. Christian men who make it an object to be rich, even under the expectation of being more useful, are very apt to impose upon themselves the truth of these proverbs: "They that will be rich fall into a temptation and a snare" (1 Timothy 6:9). "He that maketh haste to be rich shall not be innocent" (Proverbs 28:20). Great wealth is very apt to breed forgetfulness and contempt of God. In giving the power, it is very apt to induce the habits of self-indulgence and luxury. It cherishes that pride of life which is so unfriendly to the claims of the gospel. It fosters that feeling of personal independence which leads the soul to lean on earth, and not make God its refuge. It strengthens that natural attachment to the things that are seen and temporal, which renders it so hard to enter into the kingdom of God, and which it is one of the great objects of Christianity to subdue. Covetousness is idolatry. There is little room in the heart for God where it is preoccupied by the world. The love, worship, and service of God are excluded by another deity; the loyalty which ought to be felt to the Great Supreme is transferred to another sovereign. True piety itself is very apt to be stinted in its growth, and to wither away under the burning sun of prosperity; it loses its strength and healthfulness when nursed in the lap of pride and luxury. The unction perishes from the heart where it is overwhelmed by the cares and perplexities of opulence. Good men, once they become rich, find themselves insensibly attached to their gold and their merchandise, their territory and their enterprises, their influence and the splendor of their name. They become avaricious and grasping; and, before they are aware of it, they feel embarrassed in their spiritual course and find that they have new enemies to contend with, and mountains of difficulty to travel over in their heavenward career. They have little time for reading, prayer, reflection, and Christian intercourse. It is not often that you find a wealthy Christian to be a burning and shining light. I have often wondered why it is that so many who in their youth were distinguished for Christian fervor, meekness, devotion, and activity, should in middle life become so cold and languid. The simple truth is that they have become rich. Thorny cares have sprung up, and overpowered and choked the Word so that it has become unfruitful. There may be instances in which such persons become more bountiful; but it is a mistake to suppose that their liberality is an offset for their deficiencies in piety.

I would not have these remarks misunderstood. Men may be rich and yet be pious; nor are there wanting lovely examples of unostentatious and active piety among those who are the most successful in the world. And they may be pious and yet be poor, poor even to indigence. Grace can surmount the obstacles of both these extremes. But this is no evidence that our desires after the good things of this world ought not to be moderate, nor that the medium between riches and poverty is not the safest condition for fallen man. The Savior has taught us in this prayer to seek a competency in the wisdom and bounty of His providence; to seek more is neither pious nor wise. "Godliness, with contentment, is great gain; for we brought nothing into this world, and it is certain we can carry nothing out" (1 Timothy 6:6–7). God approved the prayer of Solomon because he desired a wise and understanding heart rather than riches or long life. The happiest man is he who most gratefully enjoys and makes the best use of whatever God is pleased to bestow. The providence of God is his surest estate, His bounty his best treasure, and His fatherly care his most certain and comfortable supply. He stays himself upon God, and his cheerful language is, "The Lord is my shepherd; I shall not want. He maketh me to lie down in green pastures; He leadeth me beside the still waters. He anointeth my head with oil; my cup runneth over. Surely goodness and mercy shall follow me all the days of my life!"

Such are some of the principles involved in the petition, "Give us this day our daily bread." We may well cherish the spirit of this request. It becomes us as God's creatures, and as His children. Though we may have felt His scourge, we have much to be thankful for, which we should never forget. Would that our hearts were more truly touched with a sense of His goodness! Man's ingratitude is affecting proof of his alienation from God. I had well nigh said, it is difficult to account for it, even upon the principles of his apostasy. Men feel deeply in seasons of trial; they dwell upon their losses; they magnify their afflictions; but how rarely do they dwell intensely on their mercies, and magnify the expressions of the divine bounty! How soon they forget them; what weakness and inconstancy of heart do they betray in those recollections which ought to be the most grateful and permanent! Scarcely have they received one favor but they are looking for another, and complain if it is not given. They may be slow in admitting the abstract thought that God is indebted to them; yet they too often feel and conduct themselves as though, in withholding His bounty, He was actually doing them an injury. A grateful mind is a happy mind. It is a peaceful and joyous mind. It is the zest of joy.

How little do we know of the emphasis and urgency of the request, "Give us this day our daily bread!" The stress of want compels men to pray. That prodigal who is famishing with hunger knows how to crave the crumbs that fall from the table of the divine bounty. That daughter of sorrow and want who has wept over her last loaf, and knows not, after all that her ingenuity can devise, where she is to look for the supplies of the passing hour, knows the import of the words, "Give me this day my daily bread." The time may come when, if you have never prayed before, you too may feel the import of such a request as this. Your children, too, may learn its import, and, kneeling at your feet, be taught to say, "Our Father, who art in heaven, give us this day our daily bread." And shall nothing but dependence thus realized drive you from all other resources, to God alone? Shall nothing but poverty and want lead you and them thus to pray?

Chapter 9

Prayer and Pains
"Give us this day our daily bread."

In exhibiting, as we have done in the previous chapter, some of the great principles recognized in the request, "give us this day our daily bread," we have endeavored to magnify the creature's dependence and God's bounty. We would not so represent either as to overlook the fact that God deals with men as rational and active creatures, and that, as such, they are bound to make use of their reason and their activity.

The law of reason and nature and the law of grace are in this respect perfectly coincident. Just as there ever has been a difficulty in the method of redemption by Christ Jesus in reconciling the activity of man with his dependence, so has there been a difficulty in reconciling the dependence of men on God for their daily subsistence with the necessity of effort on their part to procure it. But the oracles of God teach and insist on both these truths; they call upon men to work out their own salvation with fear and trembling, because it is God who worketh in them to will and to do of His good pleasure; and they call upon them, if they would have their daily bread, not to look for it in the neglect of those well-known laws of His providence, which He has established for their conduct in the common affairs of human life.

Man's dependence on God for his daily subsistence leaves all the motives and all the influences of human activity and enterprise precisely where it found them. No man may exercise a presumptuous confidence in the divine bounty, a confidence which gives him hope in the neglect or violation of his known duty. God is the Giver of his daily bread, but he himself has a part to act in procuring it. God's blessing is to be sought and hoped for only in the due and proper use of a man's own powers.

The purposes of God, be they what they may, are never carried into effect without the means by which they were intended to be accomplished. The means, in every instance, form an integral part of the purpose itself; they sustain, in the original arrangement of the divine mind, an indissoluble and necessary connection with the end; and without them there is no purpose formed, no end to be attained. There is the existence and influence of the great primary Cause of all things; but this does not supersede the existence and influence of numerous proximate and instrumental causes, because these latter are the selected means and instruments by which the great overruling Cause Himself has ordained the accomplishment of His purposes.

Although He is the great Giver of all temporal blessings, yet, if it is by wisely-appointed means and instruments that He gives, the application of these means and instruments is indispensable to the gift. It is so for every gift which God bestows. Men, in the common affairs of human life, never think of acting upon any other principle. There are things which God has to do in furnishing His creatures with food and raiment, and there are things which His creatures themselves have to do. The place which He occupies is one which, if He does not fill, it is in vain that they occupy the place which He assigns to them; while, if they do not occupy the intermediate places assigned to them, the series of His operations is left incomplete. With His work of beneficence they have nothing to do, save gratefully to acknowledge that it is His work; while in their own sphere, they have everything to perform, else they may not hope for His blessing upon the labor of their hands. What then, are the appointed means by which a beneficent providence supplies the temporal wants of men? Those means are mainly the following:

1. There is nothing in man's dependence that dispenses with his own industry. His dependence does not destroy the obligations under which he is placed by the law of nature; and one of these is diligence in his calling. It is so employing his time and the talents committed to him as to turn them to good account. He owes it to his Maker, to society, and to himself, to put forth his exertions to some valuable end. He who so richly endowed man with such diversified powers of body and mind, and rendered him capable in so many ways of benefiting himself and his fellow-men, has not denied him a wide and varied field wherein he may exert the powers so freely bestowed. Useful occupation is his appropriate employment; without it he will never answer the great end of his existence. Vigorous, persevering exertion commends itself to the texture and constitution of his body and mind. An unoccupied and idle man countervails all the laws of both his animal and intellectual frame, and wages war upon every organ of his material and every faculty of his immaterial being. He is like children among men; he is like the dead among the living; he buries himself alive.

If there are those who so pervert the instructions of the Bible, in regard to man's dependence and God's bounty, as to rest satisfied with praying that God would give them their daily bread without themselves working for it, there is one very ready way of rectifying their error; and the Bible furnishes it when it deliberately declares, "He that will not work, neither let him eat" (2 Timothy 3:10). It is the published law of the Redeemer's kingdom that a man must work or he shall starve.

Religion offers no bounty to idleness; her bounty is for those who would but cannot labor. If Christian liberality were regulated by the Bible, men who are able to labor, and can get anything to do, would be constrained to exertion by necessity. It is a law of Christianity, as well as nature, that drowsiness shall cover a man with rags. And it is both an equitable and a benevolent law. It is equitable because there is no equity in imposing a burden upon the industrious, which is not borne by their more idle companions; it is benevolent because in relieving men from the necessity of labor, you take from them their best heritage and sink them in irreclaimable degradation. If they would live above want, they must pay the price for it in corresponding effort, if that may be called a price which, where the habits of industry are imbibed and cherished, is itself a pleasure.

There is no relief from the operation of this wise and healthful, this equitable and benevolent law. Labor and success, effort and attainment, without some special countervailing influence, are rarely dissevered; while the few instances in which they are so form such obvious and striking exceptions that they only evince the importance of the rule. Though the race is not to the swift, nor the battle to the strong, yet is it a law which no man may trifle with, that men attain their ends by the laborious and steady pursuit of them. It is a dream of the imagination to look for a competent portion of the good things of this life without effort.

I have said that the law of labor is a benevolent law. An idle man is always a disappointed man; he is ever complaining of his misfortunes; he sinks in despondency because he is sunk in negligence and sloth. There is nothing in his eager hopes and vivid expectations that encourages and charms him. He lives only for the present, and has none of that bright impulse which carries him forward to halcyon days to come. In this respect he scarcely differs from the inferior animals; but, like them, he is environed with a dense wall beyond which he can catch but a glimmering light. His prospect is scarcely brighter or wider than theirs. The actual scenes of human life never present themselves to him in their true coloring, but are tinged with many a dark and melancholy hue. That absorbing sentimentalism, that morbid sensibility, which is so often the bane of manly and energetic qualities, find no welcome in the bosom of the man whose high aims are gratified in the prospect of responsible exertion. The primeval paradise was not sufficiently fair to make its inhabitants happy without occupation.

Man could not be deprived of a greater blessing than useful employment. If you would make him miserable, let him have nothing to do. The moral virtue of men depends, in no small degree, upon their industry and enterprise. Idleness is the nursery of crime. It is that bitter and prolific germ of which all rank and poisonous vices are the fruits. It is the source of temptation. It is the field where the enemy sows tares while men sleep. Could we trace the history of a large class of vices, we should find that they originate in the want of employment, and are brought in to supply the place which some useful employment would otherwise supply. There are others which take their rise from mere reluctance to labor, and are resorted to because those who practice and those who patronize them are too indolent to work. Idleness has slain its thousands. It is the corrupter of men and nations. It corrupted Sodom; it corrupted Nineveh; it corrupted Babylon; it corrupted Greece and Rome. The greatest (I almost said the *only*) barrier against vice is the habit of industry. Industrious habits render vice unnecessary and disagreeable, and prevent the opportunity of indulgence. An industrious man is the companion of industrious men, and has neither time nor temptation to be vicious. There is no other possible way of preventing and restraining vice in our families, in our community, in our land, in our young men, and in all ranks and orders of human society, than by promoting industry. Few men know how to make the most of human life. Time is the most valuable of all the talents entrusted to them. It is of more importance to improve human life than to extend it unimproved; to live well is better than to live long. No man can promise himself twenty years, yet may he live twenty in ten.

Nor are these unchristian thoughts, beyond the instructions of the Bible, or in any way removed from the legitimate sphere of its influence. "In the sweat of thy face shalt thou eat thy bread, until thou return to the ground" (Genesis 3:19). "Seest thou a man diligent in his business; he shall stand before kings, he shall not stand before mean men" (Proverbs 22:29). "The hand of the diligent maketh rich" (Proverbs 10:4), and shall bear rule. "Be thou diligent to know the state of thy flocks and thy herds" (Proverbs 27:23). "Diligent in business, fervent in spirit, serving the Lord" (Romans 12:11). "Six days shalt thou labor, and do all thy work" (Exodus 20:9). While, therefore, *in* all their industry men must depend on the blessing of God, they may not expect His blessing *upon* their industry. The Scriptures nowhere countenance an inactive reliance upon God, save where the opportunity and power of action are taken away. Men do not live by miracles. They have no warrant to throw themselves upon divine providence without any efforts of their own until God constrains them so to do. They should be slow to believe that such necessity exists; nor until it does exist may they cast themselves upon God without concern, and feel that they themselves have no active responsibility.

2. Another of the means, without which we may look in vain for temporal good to God as the Giver, is economy. It is scarcely less a perversion of the laws of divine providence to rely on that providence for our daily bread in the disuse of the powers and faculties which God has given us than in the perversion and abuse of the bounties He bestows. I know not how a wasteful and extravagant man can ever, with good conscience, repeat the Lord's Prayer. He who wastes what God gives him may not complain if He ceases to give.

Nature and providence are constantly reading us this lesson. One law is made to subserve a thousand purposes, and acts everywhere. Nothing is thrown away; nothing is lost; nothing but accomplishes its appropriate end. The accuracy of the divine arrangements is as truly wonderful as their bounty. In all that God does there is a place for everything, and everything is in its place; nor may this economical arrangement be disturbed by human recklessness, or even human thoughtlessness and improvidence, without suffering. This is the universal law of nature. Accurate philosophical investigations have discovered that every substance in the natural world that does not retain its original form passes into some other equally important in its place. The vessel of water which is converted into vapor and steam is again condensed, and loses not a scruple of its original weight. The billet of wood that is consumed in the fire, or the trunk that decays in the forest, gives out the whole of its substance either in the matter it deposits or the gases it emits. There is no example of the entire destruction of anything in the universe. Changes are indeed taking place in countless variety, but the most penetrating observer has not been able to discover anything that has been absolutely destroyed.

If then such is the wise economy in the kingdom of nature; if the most worthless mineral or the meanest vegetable, when decomposed, is resolved into elements which immediately enter into new combinations, and in other forms assist in carrying on the designs of providence, surely nothing was given to men to destroy. The voice of this frugal arrangement is that no man may innocently overlook this divine constitution, and either slight the gifts of providence or profusely scatter them, as if they were made only to be thrown away. And such is the voice of the Bible. Godliness is profitable to the life that now is. It gives even the lowest moral duty a place in its system of instruction. The disciple is not above his Lord. The Savior was standing in the midst of abundancc miraculously created by His command, and He chose this opportunity to give utterance to the injuction, "Gather up the fragments, that nothing be lost" (John 6:12). He did not deem it dishonorable and mean to be frugal; dishonor and meanness are more justly chargeable to waste and prodigality. He who disregards little things will be very apt to be careless of those that are greater. The foundation of wealth is laid not merely in habits of industry, but in habits of wise and persevering economy. Property is not usually acquired by a few bold successful operations, but by a slow and prudent, though always advancing process, and by minute and careful accumulations. "A good man," says the Psalmist, "will guide his affairs with discretion" (Psalm 112:5). Men must themselves not only plant and water, but watch and spare, if they expect God to give the increase. The man who makes the best use of what God gives him takes care of it that he may use it to the best advantage. His economy becomes the welcome handmaid of his benevolence; and though he may sometimes complain that it is taxed to relieve wants occasioned by the extravagance of others, he spares that he may give; the great sources of his charity are found in his retrenchments. He spares that he may spend; he lives not for the luxury of wasting.

3. Nor do we hesitate, in the next place, to specify among the means of temporal prosperity a sacred regard to the Lord's Day. The command "Remember the Sabbath day to keep it holy" is so consonant to the law of nature and or providence, and is so adapted to the wants of man as an intellectual, moral, and physical being, that he who trifles with it usually pays the penalty in temporal suffering. To rest from secular and worldly employment one-seventh part of every week, and to devote this season to the cultivation of personal, domestic, and public piety, has been found by experience to exert a benign effect on the temporal interests of men. Health of body, and cheerfulness and activity of mind, cannot be long enjoyed without this repose. The statistics have been greatly accumulated which show the fearful waste of human comfort in communities and employments where there is no such suspension from care and toil. If a man would make the most of human life for this world, to say nothing of the world to come, he will charge himself to be a conscientious observer of this consecrated day.

A little reflection will show even the most worldly men that the appointment of such a day of rest is founded in great wisdom and goodness, and that it is the interest, as well as the duty, of men to preserve it inviolate. If you look over this extended metropolis, and mark the history of those whom God has prospered in the world, you will find them, for the most part, among men who were early educated in communities and families that were taught to fear the Lord of the Sabbath. And though many of them may not at heart be pious men, yet are they men whose consciences and conduct are controlled by strong impressions of the sacredness of this holy day. There is very little hope for the prosperity of a young man who tramples upon this great institution. Had I the control of an important mercantile establishment, or a responsible pecuniary institution, I would say to a man who habitually profanes the Lord's Day, "Sir, we do not want you. There is something rotten in the character of a man who despises the Sabbath day." The parent who would see his child prosper may not fail to instill into his mind a due regard to the fourth commandment. If there are no other lessons of business which he teaches him, let him teach him this. Let a young man habitually remember the Sabbath day to keep it holy, and into what a sphere of moral influences is he at once thrown! By what a circumvallation is he surrounded that separates him from a multitude of causes that are ruinous to his temporal prosperity!

4. Another of the means of worldly good is a sacred regard to truth. Truth between man and man is the only solid basis of human intercourse. Without it there can be no confidence in the transactions of business; no order, no happiness in human society. Men scarcely know the value it gives to their character as men of the world to have it known that they speak the whole truth when it ought to be spoken; that they speak it fully and without concealment; that they speak it freely and without fear, without mincing and obscuring it, and without sinister and selfish ends, and impartially. A lying tongue is fatal to all hope of advancement in this world, as well as all hope of the life that is to come. It is in vain for a man to say that he means no harm when he utters that which is false; he does harm, and probably more than all others, to himself. Let him once imbibe the habit of uttering that which is untrue and he will find that the dishonor cleaves to him, nor can the stain easily be wiped away. There is not one, even among those who love him best and would fain contribute to his welfare, who does not esteem and love him less, and less confide in him for every instance of falsehood. A liar has no confidence in himself because he has no consciousness of an inward principle of truth and integrity in his own heart. His word is doubted; he is a suspected man; he has lost caste; he has inflicted unspeakable injury on himself; and if his daily bread is but scantily supplied, the fault is his own, the unkindness his own, and the cruelty his own. The thought may well be deeply impressed, especially on the minds of the young, that a lying tongue throw insurmountable barriers in the way of their temporal prosperity. Love, confidence, and honor or detestation, distrust, and disgrace will follow them as they are or are not observant of the claims of truth. Every unfounded statement, every misstatement, every evasive, equivocating statement, where truth is called for, every low art of concealment and dissimulation, every broken promise, serves to shut up the avenue to advancement. On the other hand, truth—pure truth with all its simplicity, loveliness, and transparency—is so usually attended with the other great oral virtues that, with God's blessing, it is the sure road to comfort, usefulness, and distinction.

Another means of temporal prosperity is that genuine rectitude and integrity of character which secure honesty in our dealings with one another. Dishonesty is one of those deliberate and sober vices, the effects of which cannot often be survived even by a thorough reformation. Sometimes it is the result of inconsiderateness, sometimes of passion, but more usually it is a calm and premeditated sin which, if it does not always indicate an advanced stage of wickedness, indicates a mind that is reckless of ultimate success in the world. A single act of indiscretion in this sensitive department of morals is very apt to demoralize the mind of the perpetrator, and lead to perpetuated wrong. He who is faithful in that which is least is faithful also in that which is much; and he who is unjust in the least is unjust also in much. Dishonesty is a sin too destructive to the well being of society, not to be ruinous to the individual who practices it. He who is willing to be poor rather than dishonest, by honesty may become rich.

5. *One more thought deserves consideration, as connected by the divine appointment with temporal prosperity: it is, a filial, respectful, and dutiful deportment towards parents.* "Honor thy father and thy mother, that thy days may be long in the land which the Lord thy God giveth thee." That this arrangement

was not exclusively applicable to the Israelites is evident from the fact that the apostle refers to it as the "first commandment with promise." For one act of dishonor to parents, the face of Ham was doomed to subjection and servitude. Where the obligations under which a child to his parents are disregarded, there is little reason to confide in the influence of any of those moral principles which are the ordinary pledge of success in secular pursuits. There are few more certain proofs of a fearfully depraved heart. This is, probably, one reason why a duty which has no proximate relation to worldly prosperity is prescribed as one of the conditions of it. But however this may be, it is one of the conditions which God Himself has established, and which none will disregard who hope to prosper. Youthful indiscretions His providence may overlook, but where this undutiful spirit and deportment are persevered in, even though repented of in later life, they are very apt to carry along with them the forfeiture of the promise contained in the fifth commandment. There stands the dreadful and unrepealed (though figurative) declaration, "The eye that mocketh at his father, and that refuseth to obey his mother, the ravens of the valley shall pick it out, and the young eagles shall eat it" (Proverbs 30:17).

Such are the ordinary means of procuring temporal blessings. Where these are faithfully adopted and pursued, men may consistently pray, "Give us this day our daily bread!" Where, in defiance of these, they are poor, God will take care of them. His hand may be upon them; sickness, infirmity, age, misfortune, may invade them; and they may be cut off from all other resources except His immediate care, and then He will care for them. They are then God's poor; and though manna may not be rained for them out of heaven, nor water gush from the rock; though their lands may not be like Gideon's fleece, nor their supplies furnished by the same miraculous Power that replenished the widow's cruse of oil and barrel of meal, this promise shall not fail: "No good thing will He withhold from them that walk uprightly" (Psalm 84:11).

I have not presented the preceding thoughts, seemingly upon a topic of purely temporal interest, without some hesitation. If any of my readers feel that they have too much to do with time and not enough with eternity; if they are repelled by them as by a cold and heartless morality, and as "savoring not the things that be of God, but the things that be of men," I entreat them to guard their own minds against all such unhallowed impressions. Nothing is further from the heart of him who pens the present chapter than thus to justify a worldly mind. I seem to hear a voice, as if from heaven, as I draw to a conclusion these secularizing thoughts, saying to the reader and the writer, "Labor not for the meat that perisheth, but for that which endureth unto everlasting life." If God and nature require care for earthly things; if they may have a place even in our daily prayers at the throne of grace, what is not required for the things that are heavenly! Oh, let us seek the bread of life; let us strive to enter into the kingdom of God! God has done much to provide temporal enjoyments; but to provide those that are heavenly, the heavens themselves have bowed, and emptied themselves of their choicest treasure. After all their industry and economy, men may fail of attaining earthly treasures; and they will disappoint them if attained. Heavenly treasures are unfailing and eternal.

Chapter 10

The Doctrine of Forgiveness
"Forgive us our debts as we forgive our debtors."

To overlook our wants, as sinners in the all-absorbing solicitude for our wants as creatures, would be as though the sentenced criminal should be mainly anxious for the conveniences and comforts of his dungeon while he neglects to seek pardon from the Sovereign to whom he has been recommended for mercy. "What shall it profit a man to gain the whole world and lose his own soul? Or what shall a man give in exchange for his soul" (Mark 8:36–37)? Of how little avail are all the luxuries of this earthly pilgrimage compared with a pacified conscience, and a tranquil hope of pardon! God is the hearer of prayer to the full extent in which the suppliant is a man of prayer. The request that He would give us day by day our daily bread may be answered in the supply of every temporal want, while, amid all the bounty and munificence of His providence, the sins of nature and of practice may be registered against us, and we remain strangers to the riches of that grace which consigns them to oblivion.

Those who are equal sharers in the enjoyments of the present world are also equal sharers in the common nature of a fallen humanity. Amid the higher distinctions of wealth and the lower degradations of poverty, neither the children of opulence nor those of want are exempt from that sweeping declaration, "There is none righteous, no, not one." When they come into the presence of that Being who levels all distinctions, the rich and the poor meet on common ground, and under a deep sense of their necessities as sinners. The day will come when they will no longer have need to ask for their daily bread. Now they are tenants of time and prisoners of hope. They have wants and may seek supply; they have sins and may crave forgiveness. The gracious and condescending Savior has put the request into their lips, "Forgive us our debts!"

The lost condition of men as sinners, as it is the melancholy fact which makes forgiveness necessary, so is it necessary to be understood in order to a right understanding of the doctrine of pardon. All that men are and have belongs to God. From Him they receive their existence; for all things they are dependent on Him. To question His claims is to do Him wrong; to resist them is rebellion. Sin is the act of robbing God. Men have taken from Him that which does not belong to them; they are His debtors; they owe Him ample reparation for the wrongs they have done, and are in debt to His equal justice. Every sinner is an infinite debtor. God is under no obligation to him; he is under all obligations to God. "Who hath first given to the Lord, and it shall be recompensed to him again; for of Him, and through Him, and to Him are all things." It is impossible for the offender to make any satisfaction; he has nothing to pay; the debt must be freely forgiven, or he must meet the rightful exactions of the avenging penalty.

Some are greater sinners than others, but all are debtors to God's justice, and stand in need of forgiveness. "If thou, Lord, shouldest mark iniquity, O Lord, who shall stand" (Psalm 130:3)? The man does not live who can deny the charge of guilt which a righteous God records against him, who can excuse or palliate it, who can make any amends for it, who can escape, resist, or endure His wrath.

"By one man," said Paul, "sin entered into the world, and death by sin; and so death passed upon all men, for that all have sinned." "By the offence of one, judgment came upon all men to condemnation." "By one man's disobedience, many were made sinners." "In Adam, all die." The fact may not be denied that the character and condition of the race were materially affected by this first apostasy. The ground was cursed on account of it. Man was doomed in all following ages to toil and sorrow, woman to be a sufferer, the race mortal, and every thing human to come into existence under the frown of an offended God. Just as the heir is ruined by the father's debt, the posterity of Adam was brought in debt to divine justice by the fault of their common parent. Just as the citizens of a state are ruined by one false step of their rulers, or of the legislators who represent them, the posterity of Adam was ruined by their divinely appointed representative.

No principle is more radical to all social organization than this, nor is there any one that is more universally recognized. Men are responsible in law for the acts of their legal representatives. A false step in the conductors of a corporate institution is visited upon every member of the corporate body. A national debt descends from generation to generation, and their posterity is rightfully bound to fulfill the obligations of their ancestors. There are also crimes of such enormity as to extend their legal forfeiture to the children of the criminal, and cut them off from honorable titles and large estate.

If we look around us, we shall see individuals and whole classes of men acting not for themselves only, but for others, and those who come after them. Their acts are not the acts of others any more than the act of Adam, in eating the forbidden fruit, is the act of his descendants; yet others are legally bound by them, and the effects of them are as truly theirs as if they themselves had performed them.

The posterity of Adam did not appoint him to act for them; that appointment had a higher origin, and is indicative of the wisdom and goodness of its divine source. If the wisdom of human laws may not be impugned for such arrangements; if men deem it essential to the interests of good government to hold one portion of society responsible for the conduct of another, why may not God, in His wisdom, legislating for all men and all ages of the world, thus throw the character and destiny of the race into the hands of their first father? The ground on which men adopt this arrangement is the common good; the best interests of the community require it. It is the best system of government; nor would it be possible for government otherwise to exert an extensively prospective influence. And the ground on which God adopts it is the same. It is not an arbitrary measure, but a most wise and benevolent one, and consults His own honor and the best interests of His extended and eternal empire. When He issued the law of paradise, He was not legislating for the locality of Eden, nor for an individual, nor for a day, but for the earth on which we dwell, for the race of man, and in all the successive ages of His history. So far from finding fault with this divine arrangement, it is no easy matter to see how it could have been different from what it was, and have been either so equitable or so wise.

Had God placed every successive individual of the race on trial for himself, what a world would this be which we would have occupied! What numberless solicitudes would have gathered around the destiny of every newborn infant, nay, what painful uncertainty, what agony indescribable till the question were decided whether he would stand or fall for eternity. And if he fell, how would those solicitudes have been augmented in view of the problem whether there were or were not any method to be revealed for his recovery! How much more wise, how much more expressive of the divine goodness, that both these questions should be decided in the person of him who was "the figure of Him that was to come," and by whose fall the way was prepared for the revelation and introduction of that method of mercy which had a simultaneous and prospective relation to the entire race; because though not practically, yet in the eye of law, they sinned in him and fell with him in his first transgression. It is easy for the mind to involve itself in webs of perplexity by considering the fall of our first parent as an isolated event in the divine government, and the law of paradise as a mere local statute; but when we regard them as the germ and foreshadowing of another and more comprehensive dispensation, both based upon the same principle of vicarious responsibility, short-sighted and fallen as we are, we may see enough in this peculiar economy not to silence our murmurings only, but to secure our admiration.

The sin of their first parent, therefore, is the first debt which stands charged to his posterity. It is not a personal, but an imputed offense. They did not, they could not, commit it because it was perpetrated before they were born; yet the legal forfeiture of it entails to them because the sovereign Lawgiver appointed him to act in their place. And though his act was not their act (nor can they repent of it, because they did not commit it), yet are they all ruined by it, made bankrupt by the defalcation of their first father.

Unsevered from the responsibility of this original sin, there is in all men the inheritance of a morally corrupted nature, constituting their native depravity. All agree that there is a fearful and tremendous visitation of the iniquity of the parent upon the children, call it by what name you will. Adam "begat a son in his own likeness," not in the likeness of his unfallen, but his fallen nature. There is not merely an utter want of original righteousness in every newborn child of the human family; there are tendencies to evil which no second causes can control, evil desires and evil dispositions which indicate that the mind is dead in sin. There are no instances of exemption from them by virtue of any natural tendency to what is right; and to whatever extent it may be counteracted, whether by providential restraint or by gracious influence, that counteraction is always in opposition to the natural bias of the mind. The history of man in all ages shows that good is not natural to the human heart; individual consciousness shows it. The mind is not even indifferent to good and evil; its predilections are in favor of evil. No child needs to be taught, persuaded, or coerced to what is wrong; while in the adoption and imitation of what is right, instruction, persuasion, the coercion of law, the authority of motives are not only requisite, but defective and inefficient.

The language of revelation on this subject is clear and decisive: "Who can bring a clean thing out of an unclean?" "Behold, I was shapen in iniquity, and in sin did my mother conceive me!" "The wicked are estranged from the womb; they go astray as soon as they be born, speaking lies." "The imagination of man's heart is evil from his youth." "Who were by nature the children of wrath, even as others."

However the mind may be improved by moral culture, this is its wretched condition until it is "born not of blood, nor of the will of the flesh, nor of the will of man, but of God." Born of man, it is human; and because it is human it is impure and sinful. That which is born of the flesh is flesh. Born of God, it partakes of another nature, a nature that is spiritual and divine; for "that which is born of the spirit is spirit." If men were not by nature totally sinful, this change would not be necessary. The fountainhead is polluted and the streams are impure. There is no moral conformity of soul to the pure image of its Maker. The understanding is darkened; the conscience has become a perverted and erring guide; the heart is corrupt; and the passions are like a stormy sea whose waters cast up mire and dirt. The thoughts are ungoverned and ungovernable; the imagination vain and corrupt; the memory reposes with gratified complacency on scenes of wickedness; the whole mind is alienated from the Author of its being and the true sources of permanent and virtuous joy. And, what is most melancholy proof of this deep-seated wickedness, these evil propensities, this antipathy to good and proneness to sin, are never entirely eradicated this side the grave, even in the best of men. When we pray "forgive us our debts," we acknowledge that we have incurred this forfeiture. There is a concession in this request that we have no righteousness inherent. How humbling, how prostrating the consideration that we are this vile!

Inseparable from this corrupt nature, there are innumerable deeds of wickedness, and overt violations of the divine law, by which men have incurred the still more fearful obligations to punitive justice. We have but to read its precepts and prohibitions, and compare our character and conduct with these high claims, in order to be convinced that the amount of our forfeitures is such as to throw us at the footstool of mercy and make us the merest beggars for forgiving grace. Everywhere men have other gods besides the living and true God; they set up idols in their hearts, even where they do not worship gods which their own hands have made. They take the name of God in vain; their lips glow with curses and imprecations of evil; they "set their mouth against the heavens, and their tongue walketh through the earth" (Psalm 73:9). They dishonor that holy day which God has ordained and blessed; they are cold and lukewarm in its duties, and neglect them for their own pleasures. Parents are unmindful of their duty to their children, and children are disrespectful and disobedient to their parents. Rulers are tyrants, and subjects are rebels against good and wholesome laws. Indifference, anger, hatred, and envy, in all the forms of outward unkindness and malignity, take the place of the charity that "believeth all things, hopeth all things, beareth all things, and never faileth." Wars and fightings, intemperance and impurity, prodigality and idleness, fraud and falsehood, avarice, cruelty and ambition, all hold a wide place in the character and conduct of men. Added to these are all the forms of ingratitude, the various shades of unbelief, the rejection of the great salvation, the resistance of the Holy Spirit, and the abuse of the divine forbearance—all and every one of them long continued, often repeated, multiplied as the stars of the firmament, and persisted in with great perseverance and obduracy.

If every sin deserves God's wrath and curse, sins like these give the divine justice imperative and resistless claims upon their perpetrators. They are righteously devoted to punishment. Sin tends to usurp God's government. He alone knows the demerit of it; nor does He ever mistake in appointing the punishment to the crime. No matter how low a man may set the mark of transgression, every sin, even the smallest, involves the nature and essence of all other sins. It is a world of sin in miniature, and only wants time and opportunity to unfold its dark imagery.

Nor is the bond that connects sin with punishment a doubtful one; it is inviolable and full of wrath. The sentence is passed, the death warrant is gone forth, and, if there is no forgiveness, the transgressor must "depart accursed into everlasting fire, prepared for the devil and his angels." It is not sovereignty that punishes, but justice, a justice which, while it never inflicts more than is deserved, may not inflict less. It is not revenge that punishes, but principle; otherwise it might change its purpose. It is not malice, for then it might be satiated; it is pure, unchanging rectitude which may not be satisfied until the transgressor receive the full reward of his deeds or takes refuge in some accepted atonement. Not only is he in debt to justice, but his arrears are continually augmented and augmenting. And it is this which unfolds to us the momentous character of the request, "forgive us our debts." For if the claim is enforced, the offender has no other way of liquidating it than by sinking under the burden in that world where the worm does not die and the fire is not quenched.

Such is man's need; and it suggests substantially the only true illustration of the doctrine of forgiveness. God is willing to forgive. He is disposed to pardon, from the infinite benevolence of His nature. Who can doubt this, who knows that He is good and does good, and that His tender mercies are over all His works? Who can doubt it, who has heard that His name is "Love"? Yet it may not be affirmed that in His mere benevolence we have any assurance of His pardoning mercy. Goodness may punish; nay, it *must* punish the ill deserving. A good law punishes, a good judge punishes, and the more certainly because they are good. However inclined to forgive the divine Lawgiver may be, and however strongly moved to acts of mercy by the tenderness of His own kind nature, justice has claims as well as clemency and compassion. And what shall countervail these rightful demands? Reason cannot; conscience dares not. The whole history of the divine government is proof that sin cannot go unpunished. The nature of the Deity forbids it because He is just and righteous as well as good and kind. His law forbids it, and stands forth a pledge to the universe that it knows no such thing as impugnity for crime. It is essential to the character of God as Lawgiver that, wherever the claims of His law are violated, His authority is enforced by the infliction of its penalty; otherwise it is no longer law, and He is no longer Lawgiver.

The inquiry recurs, therefore, with redoubled emphasis: Is there forgiveness with God? Is there any such method of mercy that does not overlook, but satisfies and honors the demands of justice? Is it possible to indemnify justice and yet pardon the transgressor? The problem is a dark and difficult one; yet, glory to God in the highest, there is a solution of it. It is possible. There is peace on earth and good will to men in the glorious gospel of Jesus Christ. The adorable God, in His unsearchable wisdom, had revealed that the infliction of the punishment upon a competent substitute is, in His gracious method of reckoning, an equivalent to the curse due transgressors. As such, it is accepted by justice in full satisfaction of all her demands; so that the repentant and believing transgressor is in this way restored to the divine favor, and pardoned through this vicarious sacrifice.

The selected system of representation, commenced under the first Adam, is thus completed under the second, the Lord from heaven. The Eternal Son, in human nature, "the just for the unjust," is "set forth a propitiation, through faith in His blood." On the revealed and simple condition of receiving Him as their Savior and Lord, His death avails for the pardon of sin. This is God's method of pardon. Because the wondrous provision for its payment originated with the clemency of the divine Creditor, and flowed from His own exhaustless treasury, the debt is very properly said to be forgiven. To us it is gratuitous; to Him it was costly. To us it is grace; to Him it was justice. To us it is gift; to Him it was ransom, a gift purchased by His own blood. The procuring cause of it is found not in the sinner, not in what he has done or can perform, but in what has been done and suffered by another.

So far as it respects the divine law, and the wrath of God as its great Guardian and Protector, the forgiveness of the offender is complete from the moment he repents and believes the gospel. "Being justified by faith, we have peace with God, through our Lord Jesus Christ . . . . There is, therefore, now no condemnation to them which are in Christ Jesus." But it is not a forgiveness that frees him from the temporary chastisements of paternal discipline, or from many a frown of his angry Father. "If his children forsake My law, and walk not in My judgments; if they break My statutes, and keep not My commandments; then will I visit their iniquity with the rod, and their transgression with stripes."

Nor yet is it a forgiveness of which the believer is always conscious. The Mary who washed the Savior's feet with her tears was pardoned before her pardon was declared; she did not know it until it was said to her, "Woman, thy sins are forgiven thee; go in peace!" Pardon does not necessarily imply the assurance of pardon. A pardoned sinner may labor under doubts and fears, and, because his faith is weak, he may not have the sense of pardon, and the comfortable intimation of it to his own soul. And this, in addition to his daily sins, is a reason why he daily prays for pardoning mercy. He would have the evidence of pardon, the pledge, the healing power of atoning blood.

It is worthy of remark that, in this prayer, the Savior says nothing of the ground of pardon, or of asking forgiveness in His name. Socinians and Unitarians have not been backward in making use of this circumstance as indicating that there is pardon for the sinner without any atonement for his sins. Yet is there a concession in the petition itself not only that we have no merit of our own, but that of ourselves we cannot procure it; we are sinners, and have nothing of our own to plead. The Socinian theory must contradict one part or other of God's word; either the representations of His grace or His righteousness. With this system, Christianity has not one principle of faith or hope in common; it has neither part nor lot with them. It was of right that God enacted the penalty of His law; it was of grace that He provided a substitute. To Christ, the pardon of His people is a debt. He can claim it as the stipulated compensation for His obedience to the death of the cross. To them it is a debt forgiven, cancelled; it is pure grace. In this petition we cast ourselves upon the mercy of God in Christ. In no one instance in all God's Word is there any promise of forgiveness, either in principle, or fact, except for Christ's sake. The Savior, at the time He taught them this prayer, left His disciples with the previous teachings, mainly of the Old Testament. The time had not come for clearer and more explicit instructions. It was subsequent to giving them this model of supplication that He said, "Hitherto ye have asked nothing in My name." They had never yet come into the divine presence upon the merit of that sacrifice actually offered, the blood of that atonement actually shed, and already fresh and flowing on the altar of justice. This is our privilege, but it was not then theirs. To us the veil of the temple has been rent in twain from the top to the bottom. Our access is indicated by the soldier's spear when it rent the divine humanity, and perforated the heart of God's only Son. We come not with the blood of bulls and of goats, but with the blood of His great sacrifice, which never loses its efficacy, which is always as it were newly shed, assuring us that we ask not in vain when we pray, "Forgive us our debts, as we forgive our debtors."

Chapter 11

Prayer for Forgiveness

"Forgive us our debts as we forgive our debtors."

Such is the doctrine of forgiveness; and it lays the foundation for prayer for forgiveness. When a guilty sinner addresses himself to the God of pardons, with the language on his lips, "Forgive us our debts, as we forgive our debtors," the matter for prayer is to be found in the instructions of God's Word in regard to the principle, the encouragement, and the great object of this request. If men are the sinful and ill-deserving creatures which the Word of God represents them to be; if Jesus Christ condescended to lay down His life as a sacrifice for their sins; and if for His sake God is the God of pardons; these are good reasons why they should repair to the throne of grace, that the effects of this sacrifice may be applied, and thus may be conveyed in all its healing powers to their own bosoms. These great truths are not only a sufficient warrant for the request, but also intimate the manner and spirit in which it should be offered.

The most superficial view of the nature and objects of prayer cannot fail to teach us that such a request as this should be offered with great seriousness of mind. We would not go into the presence of an earthly prince, even though it were to solicit an ordinary favor, without forethought and preparation; much less would we come as culprits to His throne to beg the interposition of royal prerogative in the exercise of the pardoning power without respect and reverence. In prayer we go into the presence of our Maker to solicit audience of Him whose word spake worlds into existence, and before whom "all nations are as nothing, and are counted to Him less than nothing and vanity" (Isaiah 40:17). We go to entreat Him to condescend to hear and pardon a human rebel, to plead at the throne of the King eternal, immortal, and invisible for the deliverance of the soul that will never die, from chains of darkness and vials of wrath. It is no trifling matter to hold communion with the God of heaven on such an errand as this. He is mighty to save and to destroy. If before Him angels bow and devils tremble, no sinner may take His name upon his lips, without feeling that it is a word of solemn, awful, and gracious import. If ever the soul ought to command itself into veneration and awe, it is when it comes to cast itself upon the mercy of God in Christ for the pardon of sin. To go in a careless, unprepared manner, with trifling and disrespect, or without great consideration and seriousness, or without unaffected tenderness of conscience and heart, would be to offer the prayer that is emphatically an abomination. Such requests are worse than vain oblations; they are gross insults, insolence not to be endured, were not the divine patience lengthened out even to long-suffering.

There is also an honesty of intention, a simplicity and godly sincerity, in the man who offers this request, without which he may not hope to find access. A cold, formal, listless mind when the transgressor pleads for mercy is in ill keeping with the object of his prayer. It is a guilty and sinful worm who has sinned against heaven and before God, and is no more worthy to be called His servant, much less to be accounted His child, who sues for mercy from the dread Lord of heaven and earth, and the compassionate Father of all mercies. Surely, if the heart ought ever to respond to every sentence the lips utter, it is when he is thus employed. Such a suppliant may well fill his mouth with arguments, and urge his request by all those considerations which a reflecting mind and a burdened conscience can draw from the fountains of God's truth and the riches of His grace. He will not satisfy himself with the words of prayer, but from a burdened heart will say, "I am poor and needy; O God, help me! Thou art my helper and my deliverer; make no tarrying, O my God!" The soul itself is at such seasons brought near to Him who is a Spirit, and must be worshipped in spirit and truth.

There is earnestness in the man who, touched with his lost condition as a sinner, comes in sober verity to the foot of the throne to crave pardon from a forgiving God, who bespeaks the struggles that are within. "Out of the depths," says the agonizing Psalmist, "have I cried unto Thee, O Lord. Lord, hear my voice; let Thine ears be attentive to the voice of my supplications" (Psalm 130:1–2)! The horror of the deserved curse is that which he deprecates; and if he prays as he ought, a dying man cannot be more sincere and in earnest. "Have mercy upon me, O God, according to Thy lovingkindness; according to the multitude of Thy tender mercies, blot out my transgressions" (Psalm 51:1). Yes, there is honesty, there is interest, there is awakened attention and steady thought, there is eagerness of desire, that not unfrequently express themselves in strong crying and many tears when lips of clay plead for mercy from the God of mercy. Many a deep emotion agitates the bosom then. To be in an unforgiven state is to be in a fearful state. Woe to the man whose thoughts were never engrossed by this great concern, and to whom pardon and peace, through the blood of Jesus, do not appear more important realities than all the phantoms ever crowded within the compass of this perishing world!

To be offered either in seriousness or in sincerity, this request must also be offered in penitence. Arrested attention and awakened sensibility, earnestness and agony in prayer, may not always be the sure and unfailing indices of a broken and contrite heart. Thousands have no doubt cried for mercy amid the convulsive agonies of death who died in impenitence and despair. A man may tremble under the rebukes of a terrified conscience; he may weep and turn pale at the fear of hell without shedding one tear of contrition, without one pang of godly sorrow.

Penitence implies a sense of sin, mourning on account of it, hatred of it, and turning from it unto God. The gospel is no glad tidings of great joy to those who do not feel their need of pardon. Pardon and a sense of sin that is humbling to the soul stand indissolubly coupled in the Scriptures. There is something absurd in the idea that an obdurate and impenitent mind ever truly, and in the Scriptural use of the word, prays for forgiveness. There is no such thing as an impenitent prayer for God's mercy. There may be the words, the agony, the exceedingly great and bitter cry of Esau, but there is no prayer. It would be an insult to the God of heaven for a man to pray for pardon, and yet continue to walk in the ways of sin and perdition. Such a petition would be implicitly asking God to deny Himself. Men may regret that they are sinners because they are afraid of the recompense of their wickedness; but this is sorrow for the consequences of sin. It is the sorrow of Ahab and Judas, not the sorrow of David and Peter. It is the sorrow of the world, that worketh death. It is such a sorrow as the devils have, who still love sin. There is no greater penitentiary in the universe than hell itself, yet is there no godly sorrow there. A sense of sin consists not in a bare, rational speculation or intellectual perception of the nature of sin, nor in the bitterness of grief for its consequences, but in the honest feeling of its baseness, a feeling of its base and hateful evil and not an evil in its consequences only. Nor is it an abstract view, but a sense of our own wickedness, that becomes us when we approach Him who is of purer eyes than to behold iniquity. Nor may the truth be overlooked that external acts are but a small part of that over which the penitent weeps. He is humbled on account of the sins of his heart as well as the sins of his life. Deep humiliation of soul for his past offenses, and for the present and internal power of sin, are inseparable from his every prayer for pardoning mercy.

There can be no pardon granted where this spirit is not in exercise. "He that exalteth himself shall be abased; and he that humbleth himself shall be exalted" (Matthew 23:12). "He that covereth his sins, shall not prosper; but he that confesseth and forsaketh them shall find mercy" (Proverbs 28:13). It is not befitting the great and holy God, even for the sake of His Son, to grant pardon to a man who has no true relentings of soul for his offenses. This would be to make His Son the minister of sin. Men would sin so that His grace might abound. The dispensing power of His government does not extend acts of pardon to such a man; nor has any man a right to ask for them on any such terms.

Reason, conscience, and common sense all confirm these teachings of the Bible. They teach us that there is a spirit of self-abasement which is founded on a sense of personal sinfulness, and which throws the sinner at the feet of mercy. And all the experience of godly men merely establishes these wholesome teachings. They look on Him whom they have pierced, and mourn; they are ashamed and confounded, and know not how to lift up their faces any more. They have such a humiliating conviction of their defilement as urges them to cry, "Unclean, unclean!" and such a sorrowful sense of their guilt and unworthiness as constrains them to cry out, "Behold, I am vile; what shall I answer Thee!"

It is not an inappropriate employment of the soul, before it goes thus to the mercy seat, to call itself to an account, and look into the sins whereby it has offended God. The most honest and enlightened are in the dark as to the number and magnitude of their offences, and have reason to say with the patriarch, "Make me to know my transgressions and my sins" (Job 13:23), and to acknowledge and pray with the Psalmist, "Who can understand his errors? Cleanse Thou me from secret faults" (Psalm 19:12)! The life of the honest suppliant is a life of habitual penitence; but nowhere does he exercise so true, so godly, and so deep a sorrow as when he comes near to a forgiving God, and contemplates both His majesty and mercy. There, at the throne of grace, his heart breaks; at those fountains of mercy, his tears flow. Clad with deformity, covered with filthiness, defiled with the abominations of sin that draws after it everlasting unworthiness and ill desert, he asks to be washed and made clean.

There may be those who know nothing of these impressions; there may be those who scoff at them, but they are far from the kingdom of God. Woe to the man whose sense of sin never disturbs his tranquility, never puts a check on his worldly amusements and gay diversions, never drives him to his knees to say, "God, be merciful to me a sinner!"

It is no small matter to know how to find the way to the throne of grace with the prayer for forgiveness upon our lips. The man who has not felt this difficulty has yet to learn that he is a sinner. If, as we have already seen, all our devotions, of whatever kind, must be offered to God in Christ's name, and He Himself is the altar on which every acceptable offering is laid; there is still a stronger propriety in the appointment that our supplications for pardon are offered in His name because it is only by redemption through His blood, and forgiveness of sin through the riches of His grace, that such a request could ever have been thought of. Other mercies flow through the blood of Christ, but they flow indirectly, and as the consequence of His propitiation; while the remission of the penalty of the law for sin is the immediate and direct object of His death, and that which made it necessary. The appropriate work of Christ is to take away sin and, by His bitter passion and ignominious death, to dissolve the bondage of its curse. True penitence has a living apprehension of the Lord Jesus as the Mediator and the procurer of pardon; it takes hold of the Lord Jesus as the divine and mighty sufferer; it pleads His agony and bloody sweat, His scoffs and ignominy, His thirst and abandonment, His crown of thorns, His shame and spitting, His bitter cry and His bloody cross. Here it rests its plea: "It is Christ who died." This is the sacrifice which the law honors, and with which justice is satisfied. Oh, it is an inexpressible relief to the soul burdened with sin, and bowing to the justice of the sentence that condemns it, to have the confidence that in extending pardon to the guilty there is no sacrifice of righteousness. This great atonement he does, as it were, carry with him to the mercyseat. He offers what divine justice requires; and only wonders that infinite love should have stooped so low as to provide itself the sacrifice, and permit him to offer another's life instead of his own.

The faith of prayer is the prayer of faith. Faith is reliance upon testimony, and is founded on the veracity of the witness. "This is the testimony of God, that He hath given us eternal life, and this life is in His Son" (1 John 5:11). And it is of the operation of God. There is no natural principle in the carnal mind that can produce it. It is given to the suppliant on "behalf of Christ, to believe in His name." Sin is a continual and unmingled lie, and has no affinity to God's truth. The faith which the sinner exercises in prayer honors the truth of God, and in that truth finds a sufficient warrant to deposit all his solicitude and all his burden on the Lamb of God. He has confidence in His atoning blood. Even under his greatest doubts and distress, he will not quit his hold on the God-man Mediator, nor discard his faith. He says, "Lord, none but Thee; none but Thee!"

It is a delightful thought, too, that associated as this request is with the name of Christ, it is offered in hope. Despair cannot pray. Despair has no language but its sullen and expressive silence, or its maddened shriek of agony. It is impossible to pray for pardon where pardon is hopeless. The mercy-seat is the throne of grace and the emblem of hope. No good comes of despairing of mercy. The adversary would drive the soul to despair so that he may seal its lips of supplication; he would seal the lips of supplication so that he may drive it to despair. Take away all hope of mercy, and the throne which is now so attractive to the guilty would repel them by its forbidding thunder and its flaming fires. It is only when the suppliant looks to God, not as the Holy God merely, not merely as the Lawgiver and Avenger, but as the God of love and the Father of mercies, that he comes near even to His seat, points to the sin-atoning Lamb, and says, "My Father, who art in heaven, forgive Thy rebellious, Thy guilty child!" There is a rainbow round about the throne then, and he looks up with hope. There is balm in Gilead, and a Physician there. The Spirit of adoption descends upon him, and he cries, "Abba, Father!" God will abundantly pardon. High as the heavens are above the earth, so great is His mercy towards those who fear Him. Human conception, human conjecture, and human iniquities cannot measure it. "I, even I, am He that blotteth out thy transgressions for My name's sake, and will no more remember thy sins" (Isaiah 43:25). It is not the voice of creatures which cheers the suppliant thus bowing at the throne, when it says, "Neither do I condemn thee; go and sin no more!"

Such is the spirit with which this request should be offered. “Forgive us our debts as we forgive our debtors.” It is in the exercise of this seriousness of mind, this honesty and simplicity of intention, this penitential sense of sin, this faith in the Mediator, and this hope in abounding mercy, that the sinning and guilty sons and daughters of men are encouraged to seek forgiveness from God. They need forgiveness, and they need it daily. Vain is the attempt to silence the voice of conscience, much as her remonstrances may be suppressed, and the strength of her rebukes impaired by sin. No man can practice this deception on himself with ultimate success. The God of heaven is able at any moment to fasten a sense of guilt upon him that is greater than he can bear. He can do it on the bed of languishing, under the pressure of external calamity, or in the flush of health and the heyday of cheerfulness and folly. There are a thousand ways in which He can take off the covering from the secret thoughts of men, refresh their memory in view of sins long past and long forgotten, and incite their sluggish conscience and sleeping fears. And they shall have no means to prevent reflection or divert their thoughts from the gloomy retrospect; but their wickedness, in all its forms of ugliness and horror, shall be present to their minds and haunt their imaginations like so many ill-boding messengers of avenging justice.

It would be the part of wisdom in impenitent and unpardoned men to treat conscience as a friend, to throw no obstructions in the way of her faithful scrutiny; to invite her unsparing rebuke, though she scourge them with her vituperating tongue, and lash them with her whip of scorpions. Better suffer all this than grieve the Spirit of God, become hardened through the deceitfulness of sin, and be overwhelmed with still more insupportable convictions when the day of repentance, prayer, and pardon is past.

There is hope for the man who feels that he is a sinner.

What a delightful thought that, to the writer and the reader, there is a mercy seat, and an open way to it by the blood of Jesus Christ. It is good news from heaven that "the Son of Man is come to seek and to save that which was lost," that He wounds in order to heal, that He does not break the bruised reed, nor quench the smoking flax. There is no higher, no greater goodness and mercy than the contrite and suppliant offender finds at this mercy seat. They are the highest goodness and mercy in the universe, there treasured up in Jesus Christ, and freely dispensed by Him to whoever will ask and take them.

Let none be surprised to learn that there is no forgiveness for those who do not ask it. A prayerless man is an impenitent man; and this decree never will be altered: "Except ye repent, ye shall all likewise perish." There would be no meaning in prayer if men could be saved without it. The light of heaven would be obscured, the mercy seat, itself the beauty and glory of heaven, would be tarnished, could a prayerless sinner enter into the kingdom of God. It would be a contempt of justice, an outrage on the very sanctuary of mercy.

Is the reader, then, familiar with the spirit of this request? Does he know the relief of pardon and grace? Does he know the preciousness of such a prayer? Where a sense of sin has taken hold of the conscience, much more where divine grace has bruised the heart and made it contrite, the mercy seat is indeed a covert from the tempest. Here there is redemption through the blood of Jesus, forgiveness of sins according to the riches of His grace. Let those who have not accepted this redemption be admonished that there is not the least ray of hope from any other quarter. Where the waves and billows of God's wrath go over the soul, it must take refuge in this sure and safe retreat, or suffer shipwreck for eternity.

It is the God of mercy who has taught us to pray for

mercy. It was not in vain that He sojourned here on earth, if it had been only to instruct us to say, “Forgive, as we forgive.” Having left His cross and ascended to His throne, His language is, “Him that cometh to Me I will in no wise cast out.” You will stand speechless and condemned before His throne of judgment if you do not find forgiveness at His throne of grace. Think not that such a privilege may be regarded with indifference, or such a duty deferred to a more convenient season. Do not talk of such a season. You may delay in other matters, but not here. Delay? What, delay becoming a man of prayer? Delay becoming a pardoned sinner? Delay deliverance from the burden of sin and the terrors of the law? Delay a pacified conscience, and the sweet intimations of your heavenly Father’s love? Delay going and clinging to the Ark of the Covenant, as your only hope? Millions of worlds would be no recompense for the delay of one poor

Chapter 12

A Forgiving Spirit

"Forgive us our debts as we forgive our debtors."

In speaking of the spirit with which the particular request for the forgiveness of sin should be offered, we have reserved for a separate chapter the possession of a forgiving spirit in our own bosoms. "Forgive us our debts as we forgive our debtors." As Christianity would leave no hopes for the guilty did it not reveal the truth that there is forgiveness with God for men, so it would lose its luster did it not reveal the duty of forgiveness from men to one another. A pardoned sinner is never more justly deserving of reproach than when he expresses an unforgiving spirit towards those who have injured him; and he never appears more in his true, heaven-imparted and heaven-resembling glory than when he forgives even as he himself is forgiven of God.

The language "as we forgive our debtors" cannot mean to institute a comparison between God's mercies and our own; for the disproportion is immeasurable and infinite. The injuries we receive from our fellow-men in nature, in magnitude, and in number, form the extreme contrast rather than any just and rational comparison with those which God has received from us. Forgiveness in creatures is the same in kind with forgiveness in God; while, in measure and degree, His pardon as far exceeds our own as the heavens are above the earth and the ocean exceeds the drop of dew.

The forgiveness of injuries inflicted on ourselves is not any equivalent for the mercy we ask of God, nor does it render us in any way deserving of His pardons; for this would countervail the whole spirit of the gospel, and displace the work of Christ as the only foundation of pardoning mercy. There is a very obvious distinction between the foundation of forgiveness and the revealed condition of forgiveness. Without the work of Christ no man may be forgiven, whatever may be his own personal character; while, in view and on account of His great and meritorious work, forgiveness is imparted only to a well-defined class of men. The Scriptures sometimes specify one Christian grace as the condition of forgiveness, and sometimes another. The sum and substance of their instructions on this subject are that, while no man is entitled to acceptance with God save for the Redeemer's obedience to the death of the cross, those and those only are thus entitled who are Christian men, who possess a religious and spiritual character, and are radically different from what they once were when dead in trespasses and sins. As one of the exemplifications of this general principle, a forgiving spirit holds a high and distinguished place. Other truths may be taught more frequently in the Bible, but none is taught more plainly than this, that forgiving those who have injured us, though not the meritorious condition of forgiveness from God, is that without which none obtain forgiveness. "For if ye forgive men," says the Savior, "their trespasses, your heavenly Father will also forgive you; but if ye forgive not men their trespasses, neither will your heavenly Father forgive your trespasses" (Matthew 6:14–15). Elsewhere He says, "When ye stand praying, forgive, if ye have aught against any; that your Father also which is in heaven may forgive your trespasses" (Mark 11:25). Again He says, "Blessed are the merciful, for they shall obtain mercy" (Matthew 5:7). Again it is written, "With the merciful, Thou wilt show Thyself merciful" (2 Samuel 22:26). And again, as though the

Spirit of God would sound the note of alarm on the conscience of every severe and unforgiving man, it stands recorded, "He shall have judgment without mercy that hath showed no mercy" (James 2:13).

We may be in debt to men as well as to God, and men may be indebted to us. They may have done us injury, unprovoked and flagrant injury, as we ourselves have done in forms so varied, in numbers so countless, in enormity so aggravated, to our Father who is in heaven. The spirit of forgiveness towards them is not a stoic insensibility to wrong, nor a careless indifference to the injuries inflicted upon us. This forms no part of God's character towards those who have sinned against Him. There is no being in the universe so sensitive to evil, so alive to the indignity which men have done to His nature, authority, and goodness, as that pure and holy Being to whom all sin is "that abominable thing which His soul hateth." Not to be so were connivance at iniquity, a spirit which dwells in no virtuous and honorable mind.

Nor is the spirit of forgiveness merely a restraint laid upon the angry passions, a smothering of our resentment, a mere forbearance of the outward acts of retaliation, while yet the heart prompts to revenge. There is nothing like God in this, nothing Christ-like, nothing like the Spirit of holy love, and the kindness and charity of heaven. Many a mind of lofty bearing retires, as it were, within itself, and indulges in moody silence the bitterness of its awakened and suppressed emotions of anger. This may be a dignified self-complacency in the soul's powers of endurance; it may be deceit and hypocrisy, but it is not a forgiving spirit. Many a proud and unforgiving spirit demeans itself thus, which treasures up injury in long and revengeful remembrance, wishes evil to those who have injured him, and, if he is not ready to do them evil, rejoices in their calamity.

Still less is a forgiving spirit a haughty and contemptuous disregard of those who have wronged us, as if they were beneath our notice. There may be as much malignity and revenge in the heart of such a man as in the bosom of one who demands the courtesies of social life from his equals at the mouth of a pistol, or at the point of his sword. "Proud and haughty sinner is his name who dealeth in proud wrath," one has said.

A forgiving spirit is something of loftier origin; it is a noble, generous, Christian virtue. It takes its rise in that love of God and man which is the fruit of the Spirit and the fulfilling of the law; it is made up of love and forbearance, united with the tenderness of compassion towards those who have injured us, and fortified by some just sense of our own sinfulness and need of forgiveness from God. In the full sense of the thing itself, it consists in the inward spirit of forgiveness and the outward act of reconciliation. It belongs to the heart, just as every other grace has its seat in the inner man. In this view of it, it is the opposite of revenge, which angrily seeks redress for injuries by inflicting injuries in return. It is the inward exercise of kindness and good will towards our enemies and those who have wronged us. It is an abhorrence of the wrong, yet a kind regard for the wrongdoer. It cannot be genuine unless it is accompanied with these benevolent emotions, and at a great remove from all bitterness and wrath. God requires that we forgive from the heart. Anything short of this is hypocrisy, and is accounted as such in the judgment of Him who sees not as man sees. The language of the Savior settles this point. "So likewise," says He, "shall my Heavenly Father do also unto you, if ye from your heart forgive not every one his brother their trespasses" (Matthew 18:35). The requisitions of the Bible stop nothing short of the complete concurrence of the soul in these benevolent emotions. This inward spirit ought to be always in exercise, whatever may be the character of those who have injured us, and whatever their present and future conduct. We may feel benevolently towards them without at all committing ourselves in favor of their conduct or character. They may repeat the injury they have done us every day of their lives, but this does not warrant in us the spirit of malignity or unkindness. We should love them still, and do them good as we have opportunity. It is not our place to avenge the wrong they have done, for it is written, " 'Vengeance is mine, I will repay,' saith the Lord."

In addition to this inward spirit of kindness, this constant disposition to forgive, there is also the outward act of reconciliation. Of this we must speak with more caution and discrimination, because a forgiving God here discriminates. He Himself is the great and essential Charity, and we have no desire to be more lavish in outward acts of reconciliation to our enemies than He towards His. His inward spirit of kindness towards His enemies never ceases, nor should ours cease towards our enemies. All the while they remain His enemies He is doing them good; and so should we to our enemies as we have opportunity. But He is not reconciled to them; He does not adopt them into His family, give them His complacency and confidence, and acknowledge and treat them as His friends until they have become so. Nor ought He to do this. Nor ought we thus to restore those who have injured us to our complacency and confidence, and be outwardly reconciled to them and treat them as friends, so long as they conduct themselves like enemies. The spirit of forgiveness does not require this; Jesus Christ does not require it. "If thy brother sin against thee, and return and say, 'I repent,' forgive him" (Luke 17:4). This is Christian forgiveness; this is forgiving in some faint measure as God forgives; this is placing forgiveness upon true grounds, ground corresponding with the work wrought in the heart of every Christian man by the Holy Spirit. Such forgiveness as God approves is both the expression and the evidence of a disposition produced by the power of His grace in the soul that is itself forgiven.

Our task is comparatively easy, therefore, as we proceed to show why the spirit of forgiveness in men is made a revealed condition of their obtaining forgiveness from God. The reason why a man of an unforgiving spirit cannot obtain forgiveness is that he is destitute of all true and genuine piety. The force of this remark may perhaps be the better perceived by something like the following observations.

Such a man has no true sense of his own sins. It is not necessary, after what has been said in the two previous chapters, to show that the cure of sin must be preceded by a sense of the malady, and with a humiliating conviction of personal defilement. Those who are sensible that they themselves have done so much to provoke God's displeasure, and who constantly stand in need of forgiveness, will be slow to demand retribution for the petty injuries they have received from their fellow-men. The measure which an unforgiving spirit would mete out to others would bear hard upon their own character. A due consideration of their own indebtedness would make them placable, if not suppress all desire of retaliation. The hard-hearted creditor who had just been forgiven the ten thousand talents, and who yet rigidly exacted from another the one hundred pence, and in default thereof cast his debtor into prison, justly excited the indignation of his Lord and the grief of his fellow-servants. Those cannot think very often, or reason very justly, nor feel very deeply for their own liabilities, who are so rigorously severe. It is the most lamentable of all sights to see a man who has received injury from his fellow-worm, so forgetful of his multiplied and aggravated offences against God as to go to the throne of grace and plead for the pardon of his own sins, in the spirit of revenge toward his offending brother! A sense of his own sins never could have rested with weight upon the mind of such a man; nor could he ever have felt serious and lasting solicitude for his own soul. When one fellow-worm displeases another, the latter is cold and distant; he swells in self-importance; he looks big; there must be negotiation upon negotiation, and, after all is done, there is no heart in the reconciliation. But "who art thou that thus judgest another man's servant?" No wonder if the God of justice should say to such a man, "Pay Me what thou owest!"

Nor do we see how such a man can have any true sense of the divine mercy. That he must have made a devout and humble application to the Lord Jesus for mercy, must have succeeded in his suit, and must have some grateful remembrance of those solemn transactions between the God of mercy and his own soul in order to be a Christian, all will allow.

We do pray for mercy;
And that same prayer should lead us all
To render deeds of mercy;
How shall those hope for mercy, rendering none?

How do you forgive your fellow-men who trespass against you? This is the test by which the Scriptures determine our own estimate of the boundless mercy in which God has caused us to hope. It is horrible for a man, malignant against those who have offended him, to come and ask free forgiveness from God. Satisfaction to the utmost farthing is insisted on by the rebel who, if he enjoys peace at all, must have a free pardon from Him whose mercies are great unto the heavens! An unforgiving spirit has never tasted and seen that the Lord is gracious; it is utterly inconsistent with the Christian hope. Unforgiveness belongs to the unforgiving; it belongs to those who are "hateful and hating one another." Its true and primeval residence is the region of hate, the region of hell. The devil's malice is more excusable because he gets no forgiveness. The pardoned sinner can afford to forgive, for he knows what forgiveness is. If others will have revenge, it belongs not to him. He has what no others possess: pardon from the God of pardons, forgiveness from Him whom he has provoked more than it is possible for his fellow-men to provoke him. And he has too the consolation that the approving and vigilant eye of the Lord is upon him, and that he has a refuge at His throne, which is more than a counterbalance for all that he can endure from his enemies. The throne of grace is accessible to him; but the face of the Lord is against the revengeful so that He may cut them off.

It is equally true that a man of an unforgiving spirit has no love to God in his heart. There is no surer mark or criterion by which men may determine whether they are in a state of acceptance or condemnation than love to God. And it must be owing to delusion, or the want of impartial enquiry, if any man, with the Bible in his hands, can persuade himself that love to God is compatible with an unforgiving spirit. For "he who loveth not his brother whom he hath seen, how can he love God whom he hath not seen?" (1 John 4:20).

The only thing of God which he can see and love is this creature of God whom he hates. The only thing of God which bears His image, and which God requires him to love and forgive, even as God for Christ's sake has forgiven him, is his brother against whom he is treasuring up the long arrears of malignity and revenge. "If a man say, 'I love God,' and hateth his brother, he is a liar" (1 John 4:20). Thus summarily do the Scriptures treat the man who professes to love God, yet has an unforgiving spirit. Never was man more baptized with the love of God than the disciple who made that unutterably tender appeal, "Beloved, if God so loved us, we ought also to love one another" (1 John 4:11). This is the great principle of forgiveness. If God can see anything in men to love, men may surely see something to love in one another. If He can love creatures so vile and abject, surely we, if we know anything of the love of God ourselves, can love them also. If He can overlook their faults, we can cast the mantle of heavenly charity over them, and forgive and love them still. If God's love to us, and ours to Him, were the ruling principle of our conduct towards our fellow-men, we would not find so wide a place in our hearts for suspicion and wickedness, for jealousy, hatred, and revenge. We would not find men rejoicing in the calamity of their enemies, aggravating their calamity and their offenses, and holding their persons in abhorrence. Much less would we find men in the church of God, who will not speak to each other for a whole year, dare to come and sit down together at the table of Christ and commemorate that love to which they are strangers. To injure our fellow-men is no proof of the love of God in the heart; nor is it any proof of that love to treasure up the injury.

Nor may we overlook the thought that where the spirit of forgiveness is wanting, there can be no honest regard for the interests of human society. The laws of Christ's kingdom do not allow any man to live for himself alone. He who does this, is universally despised and condemned. "Israel is an empty vine; he bringeth forth fruit to himself" (Hosea 10:1). The man of an unforgiving spirit is governed too much by a regard to himself, and too little by a regard to the happiness of others, to be a Christian man. He attaches no importance to that course of conduct which tends to make the world in which he lives the holier and the happier. The warmth of his benevolence is chilled by too keen a sensibility to his private interests. He cares not to heal the festering sores that are breaking out, and spreading their baleful infection. His is not the charity which "suffereth long, and is kind," which "is not easily provoked," and "meditates no evil," which "beareth all things, believeth all things, hopeth all things," and "seeketh not her own." Men who, for want of a spirit of kindness, can alienate themselves from the affections of those around them; who are so sensitive and irritable that they do little else than multiply enemies; who give up all the sweets of human kindness for the sake of remembering and revenging some worn out injury, and who forego all the love of friends because they will not forgive their enemies, cannot be Christians. Animosity between man and man will never cease, acrimony will never be softened to the charity of the gospel, and men united in fraternal affection, until they learn to love their enemies, and do good to them that hate them. This view of the influence of an unforgiving spirit is overlooked by the unforgiving. It is not easy for them to estimate the happiness of that community where all is kind and placable, forgiving and merciful.

The quality of mercy is not strained;
It droppeth as the gentle rain from heaven,
Upon the place beneath. It is thrice-blessed;
It blesseth him who gives, and him who takes.
Tis mightiest in the mightiest; it becomes
The sceptred monarch better than his crown.

How soon would the remembrance of injuries be effaced, and how surely followed by penitence on the one part, and tenderness and generosity on the other, were this spirit to predominate! And even if it must be that offenses come, how would their number be lessened, and their obtrusiveness and malignity mitigated! Retaliation provokes. Enmity cannot stand before love.

It would be easy to multiply illustrations of the truth that an unforgiving spirit is not the spirit of Christianity, and that a spirit of revenge is not the spirit of prayer. It is a trite saying, but has much point, that to render good for evil is God-like, good for good is man-like, evil for evil is beast-like, and evil for good is devil-like. It is the God-like we should strive after. Not all the wrath of man, nor rage of fiends, could provoke one revengeful look or angry emotion in that bosom of love and mercy. Earth and hell did their best to provoke Him to the unchanging purpose of destruction; but they could not prevent His sun from rising on the evil and on the good, nor His rain from descending on the just and on the unjust. The earth brings forth her increase, though the foot of rebellion stalks upon it. Nor could all the fury of fiends, nor the malignity of men, prevent Him from giving His Son to die, the Just One in the place of the unjust. His prayer for those who hated Him without a cause was "yet in their calamities." Even while He was stretched on the cross, amid their murderous cruelty and insulting mockeries, the last breathings of His heavenly spirit found relief from its own agonies and a palliative for their sins in the prayer, "Father, forgive them, for they know not what they do." Well has it been said, "Socrates died like a philosopher, Jesus Christ like a God." This is the true glory of our common Christianity. It would make forgiven man forgiving and happy. It would dry up the sources of his bitter wrangling, his poignant remorse, his corroding self-reproach, and his stinging shame. It would chase from his pillow those dreams of violence and blood which haunt the man on whose wrath the sun goes down, while it would fain bring angels of mercy to keep their watch over the head of the peaceful and forgiving. It would crush the scorpion within the bosom of the unforgiving, that stings him to madness. It would quench the fires that consume him, that he may no longer fan them with his own breath. It has made the only provision for the peace of men, for the peace of the world. It contemplates the universal brotherhood of man as one of its great objects; nor will its legitimate influence be duly felt until the nations "learn war no more." No man can read the New Testament without being struck with its pacific character. The visions of the Golden Age would soon return did men obey its injunctions and cease to be the avengers of wrong. A dishonest Christian, a debauched Christian, a drunken Christian, a lying Christian, is not a greater absurdity than a contentious, unforgiving Christian. Men of contention cannot be men of prayer. Men whose professional calling exposes them to stormy discussion with their fellow-men, men whose habits of life call them upon the arena of political strife, find within them too often such a state of mind as unfits them for fellowship with God. Much less can a man pray with the spirit of revenge rankling in his bosom. His conscience hesitates, his lips falter when he says, "Forgive us our trespasses, as we forgive those who trespass against us," lest he should be using the prayer against himself, and invoking a curse rather than a blessing. God will take the unforgiving at their word. The denunciations of the Bible should fall on the ear of such a man like the knell of the second death. "O thou wicked servant! shouldest thou not have had compassion on thy fellow-servant, even as I had compassion on thee?" Not satisfied with having inculcated the duty of forgiveness in a didactic form, He has put a daily prayer into our lips which, if we ourselves possess not a forgiving spirit, invokes Him to say to us as He does to the slothful servant, "Out of thine own mouth do I condemn thee!"

History furnishes an affecting illustration of the need of a spirit of forgiveness in order to retain our evidence of forgiveness from God. There was in the church at Antioch, in the third century, a minister by the name of Sapricius, and a layman by the name of Nicephorus, who after long intimacy had fallen into an unhappy quarrel, and carried it so far that they would not speak to each other when they met. After a while Nicephorus relented, and took every measure for reconciliation, but in vain. He even threw himself at the feet of his former friend and entreated forgiveness for the Lord's sake, but without effect. About this time, a new storm of persecution arose, and Sapricius was marked out as one of the victims. The magistrates ordered him to obey the Emperor and sacrifice to the heathen god. But he appeared ready to witness a good confession, and replied in an expression of his higher allegiance to the King of kings, "Perish idols, which can do neither harm nor good!" The torture was applied, and he bore it firmly. The magistrate then commanded him to be beheaded, and while he was led out to execution, Nicephorus followed him, entreating his forgiveness. But it was in vain; Sapricius's unforgiving temper remained to the last. At this juncture did the Savior make good His word, "If ye forgive not men their trespasses, neither will your heavenly Father forgive your trespasses." For at this trying period, all Sapricius's firmness forsook him; the fear of death overpowered him, he recanted, and saved his life, while seemingly on the point of seizing the crown of martyrdom. While at the same time the Savior's faithfulness was remarkably expressed towards the individual who had manifested a forgiving spirit. Nicephorus, annoyed at so unexpected a change in Sapricius, exhorted him to adhere to the faith, but in vain. And then himself flaming with zeal for the Christian cause, so dishonored, turned to the executioners and said, "I believe in the name of the Lord Jesus, whom he has renounced." This was reported to the Emperor, and Nicephorus received the crown of martyrdom! We cannot rely upon the divine mercy for ourselves, while indulging an unforgiving and unchristian spirit towards others.

Oh, that the divine pattern of our blessed Master were more constantly before the eye of His own followers! That meek and forgiving spirit of His, like "the angel standing in the sun," was the brightest of that bright assemblage of excellences that were His unequal adornment. The impressions which men receive of His religion are, to no small extent, derived from the spirit and conduct of His disciples. Hatred, ill will, and revenge are not the most convincing evidence of the power of Christianity, and in giving way to them His disciples obstruct the influence of those truths which are the power of God to salvation. While on the other hand, the kind and conciliatory spirit of the gospel, expressed especially in the forgiveness of injuries, wins over the suspicion and jealousy of its opposers, and extorts a tribute of respect, if not of admiration, for principles of such efficacy over the turbulent passions of men.

Chapter 13

Temptation Deplored
"Lead us not into temptation."

There is no lack of those who impugn the doctrine of pardon as relaxing the obligations to practical godliness. To say nothing of the absurdity of this slander upon other grounds, it is an interesting fact that, in immediate sequence to the request for pardoning mercy, the Savior puts into the lips of His disciples another request, growing out of and dictated by the spirit of the former, the object of which is to quicken and sustain their tenderness of conscience, and excite unsleeping vigilance in view of enticements to evil: "Forgive us our debts, as we forgive our debtors; and lead us not into temptation." The suppliant is not to expect pardon aside from his desires after holiness. The stronger the assurance he has of his own gracious state, the more earnest are his supplications for preventing grace. Just in the measure in which he clings to the Lord Jesus as his only hope is he conscious of this hallowed work of the Spirit in his own heart. Admitted to the divine fellowship, and with an open door into the holiest of all set before him, it is most congenial to all the affections of his renewed nature to distrust himself and take refuge in the watchful care, the preventing providence, and the restraining grace of his Father who is in heaven.

"He knoweth our frame; He remembereth that we are but dust" (Psalm 103:14). He who included the request, "Lead us not into temptation," in the compend of prayer to be daily offered by His disciples in every age of the world, must have known what is in man. It is a request indited with wonderful wisdom; a request so constantly, so universally needed, and comes home so closely to every man's business and bosom, that we know not which the more to admire, its matchless wisdom or its ineffable sympathy and tenderness.

Plain Christians, as well as men of a more philosophical turn of mind, have, as it appears to us, been sometimes perplexed by the language of this request. The Holy God is no tempter. He never corrupts men, never flatters, never deceives, never acts the part of a seducer, and never entices to evil. He makes no promises, and offers no bribes with the view of inducing men to do wrong. The word "tempt" has two significations: one is to entice to evil, the other to try or put to trial. The latter He does; the former is abhorrent to His nature. That pure and holy mind has no art, no craft, or cunning, but the most perfect and transparent honesty. He everywhere forbids sin, condemns, reproves, and punishes it; nor do His purposes or His providence, when rightly understood, ever hold a different language from this uniform spirit of His moral government. Nor is He in any way the Author or Approver of sin. As the Apostle James says, "Let no man say when he is tempted, 'I am tempted of God'; for God cannot be tempted with evil, neither tempteth He any man" (James 1:13). Ever since sin entered into the universe, He has done everything compatible with His own perfections to restrain and suppress it, to reclaim and restore fallen man.

But while He never tempts men in the sense of seducing them to evil, He tries them, and throws them into circumstances in which their character is put to the test. His government is universal and extends to everything. "He worketh all things after the counsel of His own will" (Ephesians 1:11). His providence, which is nothing less than "His most holy, wise, and powerful preserving and governing all His creatures and all their actions," to use the language of the Westminster divines, is the counterpart of His purposes, and the agency by which they are accomplished. He has, therefore, a control over all those events that exert an influence on the character and conduct of men. He is concerned in their sinful conduct, in that, for wise and holy ends, He permits it, suffering all nations to walk on in their own ways; in that He limits and restrains it, as it is written, "The wrath of man shall praise Thee, and the remainder of wrath shalt Thou restrain" (Psalm 76:10); and in that He so governs and directs it, in order to make it subserve great and important results, so that while its perpetrators think it unto evil, God means it unto good.

Nor could we have any consolation in view of the wickedness of man but for the precious truth that the providence of God is thus concerned in it all. Nor is there any evidence that the designs of God, either in regard to the Church or the world, could be accomplished, nor that the wickedness of man would not ultimately prevail and triumph, had we not the assurance that the Lord God omnipotent thus universally reigns. This every good man knows and feels, and recognizes in his prayers; and it is his happiness and joy so to do. There is a controlling power above him which nothing else controls; a supreme and universal providence over all his course; one at whose disposal are all creatures and all events, and in whose hands are all those alterations and varieties of incident and circumstance which exert such prodigious power in forming his character.

These principles and facts show us how God may tempt men without seducing them to sin, and without compromising His own rectitude and goodness. He may try them; He may put their integrity to the proof. He may even permit others to seduce them; and He Himself may place them in circumstances which shall develop their true character, show them and others what is in their hearts, make them feel their dependence, and lead them, by unexpected discoveries of their sinfulness, to go softly all their years.

Nor is there any doubt that He does this in various ways. Some He tries by the vigor, and others by the imbecility, of their physical constitution and intellectual capacity; some by health, and others by sickness; some by wealth, and others by poverty; some by the adulation of their fellow men, and some by their neglect and reproach; some by those exposures which address themselves to an ardent and sanguinary temperament, and some by those who assail the more dull and phlegmatic; some by the office they hold, the titles they bear, and the services they render to their fellow men; some by the place of their residence, the usages and habits of the society which surrounds them, the counsel of their advisers, and the varied success of their secular enterprises. These things bring out motives, and reveal secret springs of action. They bring to light easily besetting sins; and though many of them seem to be of very trivial moment, they show the utter uncertainty of all human calculations, and how absolutely the character, as well as the destiny, of men is in the hands of God.

All the changes that men meet with are trials of their character. Nero was a very different man while the pupil of Seneca, from what he was as the Emperor of Rome. Solomon was a very different man in the early part of his reign, from what he was in those voluptuous periods of his history, during which he brought such reproach upon the throne. Men do not know themselves. Hazael the subject was a very different man from Hazael the prince. Who would have thought the youthful Mary, the Queen of England, the translator of the gospels, would ever have deserved the appellation of the "bloody Mary"? Who would have supposed that Robespierre—

once so sensitive to the sufferings of his fellow men that he resigned a lucrative office under the government rather than condemn a culprit to the scaffold—would have filled Paris with blood; or that William Dodd, once so celebrated for his usefulness as a minister of Christ, would have been executed at Tyburn for forgery? Sometimes a mere change of place, an unexpected conflict with an individual or a party, an unhappy alliance in business or an unlooked for alteration in public affairs, proves a touchstone to the character, before which truth and integrity wither, and gives a blow to the spirit of self-confidence which is never so renewed that the sufferer can lift up his face before the world. Sometimes these very incidents result in a well-tested integrity and honor, prepare those who endure the trial for still severer conflicts, and furnish them for exemplary toil and sacrifices. They had this effect upon Abraham, Joseph, Nehemiah, Job, Jeremiah, Daniel, Paul, and thousands of others in later times.

The entire providence of God, and the history of every man in the world, if minutely inspected, will be found to be a series of temptations peculiarly adapted to his character. "I have led thee," God says, "to the generation of Israel in the desert. I have led thee these forty years in the wilderness, to prove thee, and to humble thee, and to see what is in thine heart, and whether thou wouldest keep My commandments or no" (Deuteronomy 8:2). He will know how thus to try and prove men, and bring out their whole hearts. They see the objects, and witness the scenes and changes by which He is trying them, but they are not always sensible of His design, nor, indeed, melancholy to confess that they always acknowledge His overruling hand. "Thou art a God that hidest Thyself, O God of Israel, the Savior" (Isaiah 45:15). Some of these tests are more severe than others, and men are on their guard against them; while most of them they seem to have no apprehension, and therefore walk on in darkness. This searching process is all the while going on, but they are unconscious of it. The trial may be designed to bring into exercise, improve, and make manifest rare graces and virtues, so that the trial of their faith may be to praise, and honor, and glory; and it may show them their weakness, and cover them with shame and sackcloth.

No one can truly adopt the language, "lead us not into temptation," who does not possess the fear and hatred of sin. The world in which we live abounds with seductive influences. It is no sin to be tempted unless we solicit the temptation. Good men are afraid of it because they are afraid of sin. This deep and inwrought sentiment is one of the great incentives to this particular request; for if the enticements to sin were not likely to lead us astray, there would be no use in the petition.

There are those who are greatly exposed to sin, and who have strongly besetting sins, who never pray that they may not be tempted to commit them; and the reason is they have no abhorrence of these sins. It gives great emphasis to such a request as this to have deep impressions of the evil and odious nature of all sin. If we make light of sin, we shall make light of temptation. One of the most subtle temptations is that which would fain induce us to believe that it is a small matter to sin against God. An enlightened and tender conscience (and much more a heart renewed by grace) looks upon sin as deadly poison. However small, it is the "cockatrice's egg," and will "break out into a viper." Every man is tempted when he "is drawn away by his own lusts and enticed. Then when lust hath conceived, it bringeth forth sin; and sin when it is finished bringeth forth death" (James 1:14–15). And it is no abortion, but vigorous full-grown death. Just as one who has experienced the agony of bodily suffering prays as no other man can pray to be delivered from pain, so he who knows by experience the evil of sinning prays as no other man can pray that he may not be led into temptation. Such a man is afraid of the opportunity of sinning; his daily prayer is that he may not be thrown in the way of it. There is no surer sign of a man's ignorance of himself than his unwillingness to admit the power of temptation. A cautious Christian has lost his self-confident courage, and seeks rather for preservatives from sin than for occasions to prove his steadfastness. He solicits rather that God would circumvent him by His providence, and on every side multiply and increase the obstacles and difficulties in his way of sinning, than suffer him to fall into temptation.

The man who offers this request with a becoming spirit contemplates his exposure. The world is full of those who have been led away by temptation, who, before they were led astray, would have said that it could have had no influence upon them. Most of the boasting among men proceeds from the want of being tried. "He that trusteth to his own heart is a fool." The spirit of self-confidence runs into temptation; it even tempts God. It should never be forgotten that a pardoned sinner is not past all peril. "Watch and pray," said the Savior, "that ye enter not into temptation; the spirit indeed is willing but the flesh is weak" (Matthew 26:41).

This exposure to sin arises principally from the following sources. In every human being this side of the grave there is a melancholy tendency to evil. To whatever extent this innate tendency to wickedness may be counteracted, it is always in opposition to the strong natural bias of the mind. His own heart is his strongest tempter. That system is a false one which teaches that it is as easy for a man to do right as to do wrong. Left to himself, he is wise to do evil, and to do good he has no knowledge. Even after every restraint and every influence, every inducement presented in the Word of God, and even large measures of His grace, he utterly fails to subdue the power of sin that dwells in him. He may feel that sin is a burden, and yet commit it. His conscience may be wrung with anguish in view of past sins, while this is no security that he may not commit them in time to come. He may form resolutions of new obedience every day he lives, and still live to groan under the body of sin and death. His very desires and efforts to mortify and subdue his corruptions furnish him with affecting indications of their power. Rarely does he go to the throne of grace but he feels the severity of the conflict, and complains of his moral corruption. It is a mournful truth that "the heart is deceitful above all things, and desperately wicked," wicked to project and perpetrate everything that is vile once all restraints are removed and strong temptation is present to the mind. No man knows what he may be left to do, nor what "earthly, sensual, devilish" device may find a place in some of the secret folds of his deeply imbedded wickedness.

The source of his exposure is not a blinded understanding merely; nor a faithless conscience, nor a treacherous memory, nor a perverted judgment, nor a wild, polluted, and incited imagination, nor the want of experience, but a corrupted heart. This is the weak spot, the sore spot, the deadly plague in the human character. He knows little of himself who does not know this melancholy truth.

Nor is this all. With such a heart as this, he is destined to live in a world of sin and snares where, whatever his condition may be, he is tempted on every side. He is exposed from the men of the world and the things of the world, from friends and foes, at home and abroad, from the untender walk of Christians, and from the bolder corruptions of the wicked; from what he sees and hears, enjoys and suffers. He is exposed sometimes from too retired a spirit, and sometimes from too social a one, and amid communications that are as contagious as they are unavoidable. He is exposed where he least suspects it, and from his very insensibility to exposure, insensibly and deceitfully conducting him from one sin to another, till he stands on the brink of the precipice, and wonders he has not made the fearful leap into the abyss below. His mind becomes familiarized with evil and, before he is aware of it, his principles become shaken, his faith shivers in the wind, and his frail bark is tossed on the dark, angry sea.

Just as matter acts upon matter, so mind acts upon mind. Disastrous revolutions are effected in the moral world by the contact of minds; nor is it at all to be wondered at that spiritual life should be jeoparded in a world that "lieth in wickedness."

There is a great deceiver, too, who is not only permitted to have the power, but is long practiced in the arts of seduction. We are not "ignorant of his devices." He knows where and when the people of God are most vulnerable. There is no dark chamber in the understanding, no unguarded outpost in the conscience, no defective spot in the heart, which he does not have his eye upon, and to which he is not fertile in expedients to find access. He sports with the understanding, and would fain tempt to the belief that there is no religion revealed from heaven, no hereafter, no God. He sports with the conscience, and would fain tempt to the belief that sin is a little matter, that the threatenings of God are unduly severe, that nothing is jeopardized by a single deviation from duty, that others have sinned and found mercy, and that there can be no great peril in sinning if such transgressors as Noah and Lot, David and Solomon, Peter and the thief on the cross, were pardoned offenders. He sports with the imagination, painting in gaudy colors the delights of the ambitious in the hope of elevation, of the avaricious in their anticipations of wealth, of the voluptuous in the revelings of their impurity. He sports with the heart, adapting his seductions to every age, every constitutional infirmity, every condition and exigency, every employment and relation in life, every hope and fear, every opinion and prejudice, every exposure, every season of rashness, and every former sin. There is no form of sinning which he fails to exhibit in its most alluring attractions: "It is fruit greatly to be desired and pleasant to the eye; the deed is soon forgotten, and never detected; it is the best if not the only means of realizing expectations to which have been devoted years of otherwise fruitless toil."

There are three things, among others, which strongly mark the temptations of this crafty adversary. One is the untiring patience by which he would persuade men to hearken to his suggestions; the indomitable perseverance by which he employs himself with their thoughts by day and by night, pursuing and worrying, hunting, and dogging his victims year after year, until he has planted his barbed arrow so deep that they despair of escaping his fury. The other, inconsistent as it may be, is the suddenness of his assaults; the unexpected fury of his onsets, giving his victims no time to deliberate, entering into no discussions with them, but summoning all his artifice and energy to carry them by surprise. And the third is to keep himself out of sight, to secrete himself from observation, from suspicion even, until the "bird is taken in the snare, and knoweth not that it is for his life."

Such are some of the more ordinary exposures to sin which this request contemplates. The world, the flesh, and the devil, these three mighty kingdoms, in all the strength and subtlety of their unhallowed alliance, are, ever and anon, directing their assaults against the men of prayer, against all men, and with an unweariedness and success that are surpassed only by Him whose eyes never slumber, and who is stronger than the strong man in his armor.

Here then we may discover what it is a Christian prays for when he says, "Lead us not into temptation." He would be delivered from the severity of this conflict; and, if he may not be free from it, he asks that he may be supported. "For this thing I besought the Lord thrice," said Paul in 2 Corinthians 12:9, "that it might depart from me; and He said unto me, 'My grace is sufficient for thee!' " This petition more especially contemplates as great an exemption from this exposure as is consistent with the designs and will of God. In the wide range between sinless perfection and absolute apostasy, some degree of exposure is unavoidable; nor does he know how much may be needful for the trial of his faith, for the proof of his integrity, for his usefulness in the world, for the conquests of divine grace, and for ultimately securing his everlasting crown. It is well that the history of the people of God in this particular is an unknown history, and that it never will be fully known till the day when the promise is made good, "To him that overcometh will I grant to sit with Me on My throne, even as I overcame, and am set down with My Father on His throne" (Revelation 3:21).

John, in the vision of the Apocalypse, heard the voice, "What are these which are arrayed in white robes, and whence came they?" It was the inquirer himself who rejoined, "These are they which came out of great tribulation, and have washed their robes, and made them white in the blood of the Lamb" (Revelation 7:14). They had labored and suffered for the gospel. They had stood firm and fast in a persecuting and degenerate age. They had not fallen nor fainted in the "hour of temptation that came upon all the earth," but sealed their testimony with their blood. God has thus tempted thousands of His people, to whom He has given grace to be faithful unto death, and to whom He has awarded a crown of life. He tempted Abraham by a command filled with all the emphasis of terror. He tempted Job and He tempted Paul. "Beloved," said the Apostle Peter to the dispersed people of God, "think it not strange concerning the fiery trial which is to you, as though some strange thing had happened to you." It is no new thing that temptations should beset them; nor is it any phenomenon in the divine government that they should be turned to good account. "There hath no temptation overtaken you," said Paul to the Corinthians, "but such as is common to man; but God is faithful, who will not suffer you to be tempted above that ye are able; but will with the temptation also make a way to escape, that ye may be able to bear it." I have known those who, from a sinful confidence in their own powers of endurance, and from a self-righteous desire to express their own meekness and submission under trials, actually desired this conflict with themselves and the powers of darkness; and I have seen them most bitterly bewail their presumption. Though good men may come unscathed from temptations, they are not to be sought. It is time enough to glory in tribulation when it comes. If God brings it, He will deliver. It is not in piety then to be a revel; she may not then resist and oppose the will of God, but "rather count it all joy when she falls into divers temptations, knowing this, that the trial of her faith worketh patience," and that it is no loss when "patience has her perfect work, entire, wanting nothing." Nor is it any strange thing that piety, when thus unavoidably exposed, should be the gainer by every seduction successfully resisted, every trial patiently endured. There is honey even in the carcass of the lion; "out of the eater comes forth meat, and out of the strong comes forth sweetness."

Thus tempted, the child of God has many a promise to sustain and comfort him. He who came from the bosom of the Father to destroy the works of the devil was Himself exposed to the impudent assaults of this spirit of all evil. If He did not escape the assault, much less may we. Like a brave prince, He not only commands His followers, but places Himself at the head of His embattled hosts, and Himself breasts the first onset of the enemy. It is not infrequently with them, after sore temptation, as it was with Him, when behold, "the devil leaveth them, and angels come and minister unto them."

While the petition, "lead us not into temptation," therefore, does not contemplate an entire exemption from temptation, it contemplates as great an exemption as is consistent with the will of our Father who is in heaven. In such a world as this, and with such a heart as dwells in man, who feels not the strong propriety, the urgent need of such a request? Nothing is more helpless than a Christian unprotected by the providence, unsupported by the grace of His heavenly Father. He is as a sickly plant under the withering tempest. He is like the lost sheep, bleating in the lone and dense forest, or trembling on the cragged rock, pursued by savage beasts and savage men, and never secure save when He who "gathers the lambs with His arm, and carries them in His bosom," makes him to "lie down in green pastures, and leadeth him beside the still waters." It is not so much in resisting temptation as in not being led into it that his safety lies.

Be this, then, the reader's prayer, "lead me not into temptation." Tread not too closely on the borders of evil when there is a "highway of holiness." Make no treaty with the foe. Beware of scenes and objects, of places, employments, and men, of feelings and fancies, which ensnare.

My soul, be on thy guard,
Ten thousand foes arise;
And hosts of sins are pressing hard
To draw thee from the skies.

If a man is doubtful of the moral rectitude of any course of conduct, let him bring it to the test by asking the question, Is it not ensnaring? Of this one thing he may be assured, that it is more than doubtful if he cannot enter upon it with the petition on his lips, "lead me not into temptation." Listen to the counsels of heavenly wisdom when they say, "Be sober, be vigilant; for your adversary the devil, as a roaring lion, goeth about seeking whom he may devour" (1 Peter 5:8). Be vigilant, because your foes are subtle, and aim their most envenomed arrows in the dark. Be sober, because levity and folly tempt the tempter. These days of temptation will soon be over; therefore "be strong in the Lord, and in the power of His might." It is not against flesh and blood alone that you are wrestling; wherefore "put on the whole armor of God, that ye may be able to withstand in the evil day."

Alas! what hourly dangers rise,
What snares beset my way!
To heaven, O let me lift my eyes,
And hourly watch and pray!

O keep me in thy heavenly way
And bid the tempter flee,
And let me never, never stray
From happiness and thee!

Chapter 14

The Dread of Sin
"But deliver us from evil."

Men may be tempted to sin, while they may foil the tempter and not only remain unhurt, but come forth from the furnace like purified gold. The evil they most fear is yielding to the suggestions and incentives of the adversary, and suffering the bitter consequences of their folly and wickedness. It is one of the most natural expressions of piety in the world, therefore, for them daily to present the request at the throne of grace, "Deliver us from evil."

It is not necessary to occupy much time in unfolding the true meaning of this request. It may not be supposed that, in offering it, the child of God prays to be delivered from all evil of every kind and degree. A measure of suffering is what he expects. He never prays, nor should he even venture to desire, to be delivered from that measure of it which his heavenly Father sees best for him. The prayer to be wholly delivered from it would be an implicit, if not expressed and direct, revolt against the revealed purpose of God, as well as against His wise and holy providence, and the discipline of that covenanted faithfulness and grace by which he is weaned from the world and fitted for his heavenly inheritance.

The design and scope of the passage show that the "evil" alluded to in this request is sin. "Lead us not into temptation, but deliver us from evil." The emphasis of the request lies in the obvious antithesis. Men are not tempted to suffering but to sin. The original word here translated "evil" is indeed of more comprehensive import, but it is quite as frequently used to denote moral evil as that which is merely physical. The Savior, in praying for His disciples, said, "I pray not that Thou wouldest take them out of the world, but that Thou wouldest keep them from the evil." He was not unwilling that they should live, labor, and suffer; He had forewarned them of this allotment; suffering was their vocation and honor; tribulation was that in which they had been taught to glory; but He prayed most fervently that they might be kept from sin, and from the power of their spiritual enemies.

So when, in this formula and compend of prayer, He instructs them to supplicate their Father who is in heaven to "deliver them from evil," He means the great evil, the ruthless enemy, the deadly plague of sin. This is the evil to which they are most exposed, which they most hate, and of which they are most afraid. This is the evil which most easily besets them, which they find the most difficult to restrain and resist, and which has the earliest, deepest, and most enduring lodging within them. This is the burden of which they most bitterly complain; heavier than losses, more distressing than sickness, more mournful than sorrow, more severe than persecution, more withering than reproach, and more galling than chains. This is the enemy with which they are called to maintain a sleepless and perpetual warfare because it contends for the throne in their hearts, because if it is let alone it will live and reign in the soul forever, and because it never dies save a lingering, painful, and excruciating death. This is the sea of trouble whose dark waters roll over them, and which, though often buffeted and repelled, may return from some unexpected source and in some new channel, and sink them in the depths. They can welcome anything rather than this. There is nothing that is the source of so much depression and discouragement as this great evil. It costs them tears, groans, and prayers.

"Mine iniquities," said the Psalmist, "are gone over my head; as an heavy burden, they are too heavy for me. I am troubled, I am bowed down greatly; I go mourning all the day long. I am feeble and sore broken; I have roared by reason of the disquietude of my heart" (Psalm 38:4–8)! Many a time are they constrained to exclaim with Paul, "O wretched man that I am! who shall deliver me from the body of this death?"

One of the most effective means of deliverance from this great evil, is prayer. There are, it is true, other means. Temptation must be avoided; evil pursuits, evil associations, and all corrupting influences must be put far away. We must realize more deeply our obligations to God. We must labor for a deeper sense of the vanity of this world, and more abiding impressions of the world to come. We must dwell often and tenderly on the love and sufferings of our great atoning and interceding High Priest. We must acquaint ourselves more with God, habitually feel that we are always in His presence, be cheerfully employed in our duty, and make it our high ambition always to do those things which are well pleasing in his sight who sees us everywhere, and from whose presence none can flee. But the great encouragement, stimulus, and relief in all these efforts is derived from prayer. Sin cannot be mortified without prayer, because it cannot be mortified without a power superior to our own, the power of God's gracious, condescending, and omnipotent Spirit. "If ye, through the Spirit, do mortify the deeds of the body, ye shall live" (Romans 8:13).

No man ever engaged in a successful conflict with his corruptions without feeling his dependence on God, and his need of the Holy Spirit, to give him the victory over even one sin. Without this, nothing is accomplished; the besetting sin gains strength; all sin has augmented power; and, instead of being delivered from evil, the most holy men, so far from making any advances in the divine life, would wax worse and worse.

We frequently read in the Scriptures of the throne of grace as the refuge of God's people in the time of trouble. And what a refuge it is when, from the storms of earth, they hide themselves in His pavilion! Nor is it more a refuge from their sorrows, privations, and tribulations than a refuge from their sins. If true believers in Jesus had a more intimate acquaintance with one another's experience, it would probably be found that there is no one blessing for which they prize the throne of grace more than this. Multitudes are found among them who can say, "Sin had been a pleasure and religion a burden but for the privilege of prayer. I had been among the vilest of men but for a throne of grace. Long ago had I been in hell with the damned but for a throne of grace." It is here that the soul not only finds pardon for the past, but strength for the present, and bright kindlings of hope for the future. It is here that she is brought into contact not with things that are evil, but things that are good. It is here that she perceives the beauties of holiness, takes hold of the divine strength and the divine promises, feels that her life is hidden with Christ in God, and, while she goes on her way, rejoices as she goes.

There are important reasons for this special request, "deliver us from evil." True religion is as reasonable as it is lovely. Though with every child of God such a request is in no small degree a matter of feeling, yet are its weight and importance enforced by every dictate of reason and conscience as well as every emotion of piety. Let us direct our thoughts in the subsequent part of this chapter to a consideration of the question, Why do the children of God thus fervently pray to be delivered from sin?

Sin is itself exceedingly sinful. It is an evil thing and bitter. It is the poisoned arrow, the dart that most bitterly wounds the soul. One of the points of difference between those who are Christians and those who are not will be found to consist in their different views of sin. Good men view it in some measure as God Himself views it. The reason why God hates and forbids it is that it is wrong. It is opposed to His nature and a violation of His law. It is eminently the "accursed thing," and that which His soul hates. He is of purer eyes than to behold evil, and cannot look on iniquity. He is not opposed to it because He is afraid it will injure Himself, though it is enmity against Him, and all its tendencies are to frustrate His designs and subvert His throne. "If thou sinnest, what doest thou against Him? Or if thy transgressions be multiplied, what doest thou unto Him" (Job 35:6)? His nature remains spotless, and His blessedness undisturbed; His counsel shall stand, His throne endure forever, and He will even make the wrath of man praise Him. Yet is there nothing more repugnant to Him, as a Being of perfect rectitude, than this abominable, odious thing. He has a quick, instinctive, and unchanging sense of what is right. It is a matter of principle with Him; nor can it be otherwise than that He should be the everlasting Enemy of sin.

When men are born of God and become His children, they imbibe a portion of His nature and Spirit. Because sin is odious in itself and hateful to Him, it is hateful to them. The time was when they regarded it otherwise, but that time has gone by. All the sensibilities of their renewed nature are now wounded by it, and it is their earnest prayer that they may be delivered from its power. It is all evil; they see no good in it. It is the fountain of corruption. It makes the devil evil; it makes the human heart evil; it makes the world evil. They themselves know the pain and the grief of being brought under its dominion; they have a painful sense of its turpitude. Many a time have they been subdued to tenderness and tears, and have wept and bled, on account of it.

It is not like other evils which come upon them, and

which they mourn over, but which have no moral turpitude. Sickness and poverty, pain and death, are evils, but they are not sins. The consuming flame, the desolating flood, grim famine, and the withering thunderbolt are evils; but they are not sins. They never sting the conscience; there is some relief in contemplating these; but, save in the blood of Christ, there is none in contemplating sin. It has no excuse, no palliation. Whatever it touches, it corrupts and makes evil. It has no resemblance to what is right, no one element of purity and loveliness. In its best forms and least enormity, it is crime, dire and direful crime. With all its meretricious adornment, it is an evil which conscience revolts at, from which every virtuous mind shrinks, and from which He who once bore its mighty burden and shame has well taught His disciples to implore deliverance.

There is also debasement and shame in sin as well as moral turpitude. The soul of man was originally pure and holy; it was the most amiable and beautiful object in this lower world, but a little lower than the angels, formed in the image of its Maker, lofty, lovely, and justly beloved. It was endowed with high intellectual faculties, with a sound and healthy conscience, with affections pure as the crystal stream. All its parts were fitly joined together, and all its separate functions maintained that due subservience and subordination which constituted it a harmonious spiritual existence. If the love of the beautiful, the admiration for the sublime, could be gratified with perceptions of what was pleasing and grand in the newly completed material creation, much more were they gratified with this highest, noblest, and honored work of God.

It is among the basest and worst features of sin that it defiles and pollutes the soul, once so pure and honored. When man fell, this pure and lofty existence became deteriorated and depraved; its faculties were deranged, its harmony disturbed, and its beauty defaced, its glory turned into shame. It became diseased and defiled—a pale, sickly, debased existence. When through matchless grace it is born of God, and created anew in Christ Jesus, it begins to assume its primeval beauty, to put on its vestal robes, and to shine forth in its original loveliness. Its symmetry is restored and its disjointed and jarring faculties once more act in harmony. It makes progressive advances in holiness; habitually, though inconstantly, it is tending upward, till ultimately it attains to that unblotted excellence which was once its highest glory.

To this upward progress sin opposes the most humiliating obstacles; it acts upon the mind just as a stupefying or inflammatory disease acts upon the body. To a greater or lesser extent, every sin does this; while habitual and aggravated sin does it to an alarming degree. The heart, the great moral principle, the master impulse of the wondrous machinery, itself disordered, throws into disorder all the natural faculties. The understanding becomes darkened, the judgment confounded, and reason itself no longer compares, compounds, and arranges as a well-balanced mind is wont to do, but plunges into the deepest and most foolish absurdities. The beauty, excellence, and glory of God and divine things fade from the mind, or are seen through a false medium. Spiritual things are no longer compared with spiritual; natural things are no longer seen in their moral relations; the views of the mind are blind and partial, and it is warped to conclusions that are false and unrighteous. Memory too becomes most treacherous where it ought to be most faithful, and, instead of being the repository of thoughts that are true and heavenly, becomes the store-house of all that is earthly, and not a little that is sensual and devilish. Conscience becomes misinformed, misled, bribed, and stifled, or, where it rises above these errors, brings the soul into terror and bondage.

This view of the evil of sin may not impress the minds of

all good men alike; but there are those to whom it is a most humiliating view. They are conscious of the defilement of sin; it is a melancholy, debasing consciousness. It despoils them of their glory, and leaves them in their nakedness and shame. It is like the plague of leprosy: it covers the soul; it is too polluting and contagious to go abroad without some badge of its uncleanness. There is nothing in it that is pure and honorable. It is a loathsome, filthy disease; and the man who is polluted by it does well when he covers his face and clothes himself with sackcloth.

When the children of God are conscious of having fallen into sin, even after their gracious healing, they feel oppressed with that humiliating sense of their vileness which extorts from their bosoms the confession, "Unclean! unclean!" The prophet's acknowledgment was, "O my God, I am ashamed and blush to lift up my face to Thee, my God" (Ezra 9:6)! "O Lord, righteousness belongeth unto Thee; but unto us confusion of faces" (Daniel 9:7)! It is no marvel that the daily prayer should go up to the throne, "Wash me thoroughly from mine iniquity, and cleanse me from my sin!" The pollution of sin is often felt to be deeply odious and degrading; in no words is the humbling sense of it more fully expressed than in the short sentence, "Behold, I am vile!" However prosperous their outward condition, and however many and expressive the tokens of confidence they receive from their fellow-men, nothing satisfies the people of God but to be delivered from evil. They have no stronger desire, no prayer more importunate, than that the body of sin might be destroyed, so that henceforth they should not serve sin. Their daily application is to the blood that cleanses, and their daily request is that God would heal their backslidings.

It is worthy of remark that, amid all the philosophical theories in regard to the ultimate good which sin is made to subserve, men of prayer are not embarrassed with theories on so plain a subject. They do not stop to ask if God may not glorify Himself by their wickedness; sin is too odious to allow of any such palliations. In defiance of all theory, the Spirit of God has taught them its exceeding defilement, and they cannot help praying to be delivered from its pollutions. Every emotion of piety prompts them thus to pray; the mere impulse of right affection overpowers all their nice metaphysical distinctions and subtleties, and constrains them to implore, "Lead us not into temptation, but deliver us from evil."

There is also suffering in sin as well as evil and shame. In piety there are joys. Angels find them in the pure and devout affections of their own minds, in their delighted contemplations of their adored Author and Sovereign, in their admiring views of His works and providence, in their growing conceptions of His great work of redeeming mercy, in their fellowship with God, and in His favor and love. The lowest and meanest seraph is indeed happier in these sources of joy than the highest and most exalted child of God on earth; yet the lowest and meanest child of God on earth has spiritual enjoyments such as no man takes from him.

True religion, wherever it is felt in purity and power, always produces the most happy effect upon the mind that embraces it. It is the Sun of righteousness arising upon the soul after the darkness of a long and gloomy night. It is like the returning spring, melting the ice and dispelling the chill frosts of winter, giving life to the buried seed, clothing it with verdure, and spangling it with flowers. It spreads serenity and joy over the very countenance, lights up the languid eye, and fills the lips with praise. Not more certainly is it the life of God in the soul of man than it imparts a portion of the very blessedness of God to the soul itself. "To be carnally minded is death, but to be spiritually minded is life and peace" (Romans 8:6).

There is a love of God, a confidence and hope in God, a communion and fellowship with God, which not only lead the soul to stay itself upon Him, and feel safe and tranquil, but which fill it with triumph. "Thou hast turned from me my mourning into dancing," said the Psalmist. "Thou hast put off my sackcloth and girded me with gladness, to the end that my glory may sing praise unto Thee, and not be silent" (Psalm 30:11–12).

Nor is there anything that prevents these joys from being constant, unless it is the chilling, withering influence of sin. Sin is the atmosphere of death. It is like returning winter to the soul when sinful thoughts, sinful passions, and sinful pursuits agitate it. They sweep over its calm surface, and upturn the deep foundations of its joy. They make it restless and unhappy, and, if their influence is permanent, render it like a frozen ocean where the ice of centuries has been accumulating, and every current of air that comes from it chills and freezes. The light of the divine countenance is withdrawn from it by day, and God its Maker no longer gives it songs in the night. Gloom and darkness hang over it. Its garments of gladness are laid aside, and it puts on its weeds. It has no longer that comfortable evidence of its interest in the divine favor which made it joyful in the house of prayer. Deserted of all but unbelieving doubts, cruel fears, a guilty conscience, and bitter lamentations, it is well nigh abandoned to its invisible enemies and sinks into morbid dejection and melancholy.

The Christian who is even surprised into sin finds it difficult to return to his wonted enjoyment of God. They are suppressed aspirations of heart towards Him which he feels rising in his bosom; he is embarrassed in his fellowship; his access in the new and living way is obstructed; he feels for a time like a stranger and foreigner, an outcast, rather than like the happy child of God. He has no comfort in prayer; no light shines upon the sacred pages of God's Word when he opens that sacred volume; no promise meets his uncomforted heart; ordinances are barren; and in the bitterness of his soul, he is ready to exclaim, "God has forgotten to be gracious; He hath in anger shut up His tender mercies" (Psalm 77:9).

A wicked man, a self-deceived man, a vile hypocrite, can live in such a state of mind as this, so far as he knows what such a state of mind is; but it is a state of mind which no Christian can long endure. Things seen and temporal cannot make him happy while he is thus shut out from things unseen and eternal. He cannot live thus abandoned of God; he would welcome death in the assured peace with his heavenly Father rather than life under the sorrows of this spiritual desertion.

It is not without reason, therefore, that he prays against the invasions of sin from without and the indulgence of sin within, "Cast me not away from Thy presence; take not Thy Holy Spirit from me" (Psalm 51:11). His very sorrows and griefs find their consolation in the prayer to be delivered from evil.

Sin also diminishes, if it does not destroy, the Christian's usefulness. True piety is efficient and operative. The great object of every Christian is to live not to himself, but to Him who died for him, and rose again. But it should never be forgotten that the value of his religious character is derived from its moral influence. Nowhere is this unquestioned influence more exerted than in those humble efforts, those cheerful acts of self-denial, those unreluctant sacrifices, and that unnoticed toil and patient perseverance in well doing, which have the promise of reaping in due season.

Sin, more especially indulged sin, is ruinous to his influence and usefulness. If even the heaven born Paul complained that his sins interrupted him in the performance of his duty, who and where is the saint who does not discover reasons for the prayer, "Deliver me from evil"? "I am carnal," said this peerless apostle, "sold under sin. For that which I do, I allow not; for what I would, that do I not; but what I hate, that do I. I find then a law that, when I would do good, evil is present with me" (Romans 7:20–21). He was conscious of a conflict, the severity of which sometimes unfitted him for those arduous and self-denying duties, and those wondrous enterprises of Christian heroism which were the objects of his high wrought and holy zeal. He was afraid of sin, because he well knew its tendency to paralyze his usefulness. Those who possess most of the spirit of Paul, for the same reason, "groan, being burdened." It is an afflictive thought to them ever to be in a state of mind in which their duty is irksome, their courage prostrated by self-reproach, or the reproach of their fellow men. "Then shall I not be ashamed," said the Psalmist, "when I have respect unto all Thy commandments" (Psalm 119:6). When good men, by their own folly and backsliding, have brought opprobrium upon the sacred name by which they are called, when they have thrown stumbling blocks in the way of those who are without, and not only given occasion to infidels and scoffers to triumph over their fall, and to speak even more lightly than they are wont to do of the religion of the Bible, but have also furnished reason for the friends of God to suspect their sincerity; they know not how to lift up their faces, they are humbled and distressed, and not infrequently court retirement and solitude, rather than spheres of active usefulness. Even if their sins are secret, they feel a shrinking reluctance at occupying places of consideration and influence. Christian usefulness is a plant of slow growth: it spreads itself gradually; yet if there creeps in a worm at the root, it withers more rapidly than it grew. The usefulness of a good man is inseparably connected with the views which men have of his religious character. Their respect for him gives energy to his efforts. Men of no great strength of purpose or vigor of effort are not infrequently in no common degree useful because they are, confessedly, very good men. Where a good man has palpable and glaring sins; where his character is such that, though his fellow-men do not deny him the credit of being a Christian, those who know him best respect and love him least, he may not hope to be eminently useful.

Though every true Christian desires more to be a child of God than to seem to be such, it is not unbefitting the truest sincerity and the truest humility that he should desire so to conduct himself that his fellow men may have confidence in his piety. Nothing less than this is required of him by the Savior when He utters the injunction, "Let your light so shine before men that they, seeing your good works, may glorify your Father who is in heaven" (Matthew 5:16). He should be watchful that nothing he says or does, and nothing he leaves undone or unsaid, shall destroy, or even diminish, the good influence he might otherwise exert.

And is it any marvel that such a man should sometimes fear and tremble? Is it wonderful that he should often employ his thoughts in faithful self-inspection; that he should sit in severe judgment upon his own heart and character; that his daily prayer should be, "Hold Thou me up, and I shall be safe! Deliver me from evil!"

Another reason for this request is found in the fact that sin is so universally destructive in its tendencies upon the happiness and best interests of the world in which we dwell. We may only glance at this prolific and mournful thought. The ravages of sin may be traced in all the course it has trodden from the fall of angels to the present hour. There is no form of happiness that has not withered at its approach, none of misery and woe, be they ever so varied and hideous, that have not followed in its train. It has made the human bosom, otherwise tranquil and unruffled, the seat of conflict, and agitated it by storms. It has drowned the hopes of men in an ocean of fears. Throughout the length and breadth of this wide world it has dug its valley of tears, and overhung it by the shadows of death. Its emblems are hung round the dungeon and the stake, the prison and the gallows; they are suspended over every battle-field, and intermingled with every convulsion that has passed with confused noise over the earth.

Go to the bowels of the earth and the channels of the sea, and there are its triumphs; it has made sea and land a world of graves. It kills the body and damns the soul. It created the walls of that gloomy prison, whose broad gateway bears the inscription, "Where the worm dieth not and the fire is not quenched." There it confines the rebel angels; there it conducted Sodom and Gomorrah; there it hurled Pharaoh and Babylon; and there its burning, malignant fury remains unquenched. Ruined legions emit thence the memorable warning, "Beware of sin!" and were they still prisoners of hope they would say, "Deliver us from evil!"

There is still another reason for this request; it is found in the claims of redeeming love. The suppliant is one who addresses the God of pardon. He has become reconciled to Him through that mighty Sufferer who hung upon the cross. God is his Father now; he would not wound that heart of paternal love. More powerful than the obligations of the law, the love of God and the love of the cross attracts him. It is not fear that moves him so much as love. "Perfect love casteth out fear"; and though his love is far from perfect, yet is it stronger than those chains of darkness at which he once trembled, more potent than the fiery walls of that eternal prison which once filled him with terror, and by its resistless bands draws him every day to his Father's mercy seat to supplicate, "Deliver me from evil." His heart is burdened with the desire that he may have no fellowship with the cruel, accursed thing that tore the much loved One from the tranquil bosom of heaven, dragged Him down to the degradation of a creature, the servitude of a slave, and shamelessly nailed Him to the cross. Sin was the crime perpetrated in the holy empire of the Most High that could not be atoned for, save by the eternal agonies of the perpetrator or the crucifixion of the eternal Son of God; and shall he not hate it? Shall he not pray to be delivered from its power? Thousands of rams and ten thousand rivers of oil could not make amends for it; and shall he not bewail its malignity? Go forth, O my soul, and see what sin has done! Look away to Calvary, and there read and learn the never-to-be-forgotten lesson. Go on those bended knees before the throne of mercy, and when, in the peaceful and heaven imparted spirit of adoption, you can say, "My Father, who art in heaven," say also, "Deliver me from evil!"

Something like the preceding views are those of every true believer in giving utterance to this emphatic request. The conflict of such a man with sin is very different from the mere struggles of natural conscience. Wicked men are not strangers to this conflict in some sort; yet while their conscience struggles against it, they do not feel it to be their burden, but are still controlled by the love of sinning. The struggles of natural conscience are occasional and partial, while the Christian's conflict with sin is habitual. His warfare is with the whole body of sin; nor does he cease from the conflict until at last he gains the victory. Natural conscience wages war mainly with outward sins, while true piety watches, with eagle eye, the secret evils of the heart, and contends with sins known only to the all-seeing Witness and Judge. The believer hates sin; the unbeliever fears it, and only with the servile fear of punishment. The believer resists it from principles unknown to mere natural conscience. He contends with it by faith and prayer, and in humble dependence on his Father who is in heaven; while natural conscience leaves out of sight the grace to help. When a good man sins, his conscience ultimately becomes more sensitive and faithful; he dreads the approaches to sin as the burned child dreads the fire; while experience and observation show that the more a wicked man sins, the more his conscience becomes callous and seared. Judas felt the scorpion sting of a wounded conscience; Peter felt the pangs of a broken and contrite spirit.

This petition in the Lord's Prayer, therefore, furnishes one of the criteria by which every man may judge his spiritual state. Could you listen when a thoughtless sinner prays, you might hear professions of thankfulness, requests for the divine bounty, and deprecations of the coming wrath; but few, if any, supplications are there to be delivered from sin. Could your ear be open when the child of God enters into his closet and shuts the door, you would hear what, in the ears of the men of the world, might seem to be strange requests. You would, indeed, hear the song of thanksgiving and the pleadings of a broken heart for pardoning mercy, but you would hear solicitations still more fervent to be delivered from evil. Nay, in the seasons of his greatest fervor and spirituality, such a man might rise from his knees without once uttering the request, "Give us this day our daily bread," while he would never forget to implore that God would keep him from sin, and make him more and more conformed to the image of His Son. Another day will show if the reader has this spirit, and thus indicate whether he is or is not a child of God.

I have said that the Christian's struggle with sin is no momentary conflict. Nor is it an unsuccessful one. He may not gain every battle; he may, indeed, sometimes fall, and be found bruised, maimed, and bleeding on the field; but he shall at last come off more than a conqueror through Him who loved him. "In the world ye shall have tribulation; but be of good cheer, I have overcome the world" (John 16:33). Spiritual affections may languish and decline, but they shall not die. It would be a dark sign if the Christian were satisfied with his present attainments. Let him take courage in the thought that iniquity shall not be his ruin. He is not of those who draw back to perdition, but of those who believe to the saving of the soul. Let him study to prove himself a good soldier of Christ. Let him seek to know not how he may cover his sin, but how he may detect it, and how it may be subdued. He can do all things through Christ who strengthens him.

There are those who trifle with sin. They trifle with it in their thoughts; they speak lightly of it; they excuse and extenuate it; they commit it without remorse; and they rejoice and triumph when they discover it in themselves and in their fellow men. Never was there a deeper infatuation than this. "Fools make a mock at sin" (Proverbs 14:9). Nothing remains for such a man but indignation and wrath, tribulation and anguish. Sin is his enemy. It will be a miracle of mercy if it does not give malignity to the undying worm and ignite the fires that never shall be quenched.

Should these pages fall into the hands of anyone this insensitive and infatuated, let him stop in his mad career before he makes the fearful plunge into the world of retribution; let him look on Him whom he has pierced, and mourn. Even now, the throne of grace invites him to bow at its footstool in self-abasement and tears. No prayer is more befitting such a man than this last request, in that form of prayer which Christ taught His disciples, "Deliver me from evil." Let him break off his iniquity by righteousness, and his transgressions by turning to God. Let him repair to the fountain opened for sin and uncleanness, and say, "Purge me with hyssop, and I shall be clean; wash me, and I shall be whiter than snow." Let him go at once; let him fill his mouth with arguments; let him urge his way through obstacle and snare; let him boldly and fearlessly come near the throne! Oh, what is this I am saying? Let him rather, like the publican who, "standing afar off, durst not lift his eyes to heaven," smite upon his breast, and say, "God, be merciful to me, a sinner!"

Chapter 15

The Argument by Which Prayer is Enforced
"For Thine is the kingdom, and the power, and the glory forever, Amen."

We feel no small degree of reluctance in dismissing our contemplations upon this inimitable prayer. In bringing our meditations upon it to a close, our emotions are not unlike those the Christian feels in the more favored seasons when he has climbed the mount of prayer, and with lingering and tardy steps turns again to mingle with the noisy and bustling world. Thought crowds upon thought in his supplications; emotion swells upon emotion; and his suppressed yet reiterated "Amen," while it speaks the satisfaction of his heart at the throne of grace, also tells its sadness that he must mingle with other and less hallowed scenes.

Our regret at arriving so soon at the close of these meditations is, however, not a little relieved by the richness and variety of the topics on which we are allowed to dwell in these closing thoughts. When Christ undertakes to teach us, the instruction is complete. He will not have our petitions abrupt in their beginning, nor altogether unceremonious in their conclusion. We should approach the mercy seat recognizing His kindness, His tenderness, and His greatness, and leave it acknowledging our dependence upon Him for all we desire and expect. "For Thine is the kingdom, the power, and the glory forever, Amen."

In attempting to unfold and impress the spirit of this concluding sentence, we may not overlook the force of the conjunctive word "for," with which it begins; this is the true key to the whole passage. "*For* Thine is the kingdom, the power, and the glory." This is the reason urged by the suppliants why the request so comprehensively set forth, and embodying objects of such magnitude, should be granted. In offering them, they solicit no common favors; they open their mouth wide so that God may fill it. They ask for nothing less than that the name of their Father who is in heaven may be hallowed, that His kingdom may come, that His will may be done on earth as it is in heaven, that He would furnish them with the daily supply of all their wants, that He would pardon all their sins, that He would not lead them into temptation, and that He would deliver them from evil. There is great compass of thought and desire in such requests. What encouragement, what warrant even, have sinning men for offering them? By what arguments can they urge such petitions, and what reason they have to look for favorable and gracious answers to their supplication!

They are weighty and effective reasons. The kingdom, the power, and the glory belong to the great and gracious Being addressed, and belong to Him forever. They do not pray to the idols of the heathen, who are the work of men's hands, nor to men who are as powerless as themselves, nor to saints, nor angels, nor yet the highly favored mother of the incarnate Jesus, who have neither kingdom, nor glory, nor any power save such as God is pleased to give them. The object of their supplications is their Father who is in heaven. It is not merely to all that is affectionate, kind, and condescending in His paternal character that they make their appeal, but to all that is great and glorious. It is to the King eternal, immortal, and invisible; to the Lord God Almighty; to the Father of glory as well as the Father of mercies, and their Father who is in heaven.

Prayer is not the unmeaning utterance of the lips, nor the

effort of an unthinking mind. There is strong propriety, there is even importance in urging our requests at the throne of grace by reason and argument. We are taught by the Apostle James that "the effectual, fervent prayer of a righteous man availeth much." With whom does it avail? Not with the suppliant, for he is the person who prays, and not the person to whom prayer is addressed. It has been more generally believed that the true and proper design of prayer is to produce an effect on the suppliant by bringing into exercise the graces of his renewed nature, and securing such a state of mind as God shall approve, and to which He will grant that expression of His approbation implied in answers to prayer. No doubt that this is one of the effects of prayer; but the very idea of prayer carries with it the idea that its design is to act upon the mind of the Being to whom it is addressed. Nor, so far as I can recall the instructions of the Bible, is there a single sentence or suggestion that the great object of prayer is to produce a fitting state of mind in the suppliant to receive the blessing he solicits; the Being prayed to is God Himself. Nor is the language too strong to say that the design of praying to Him is to influence and induce Him to give what we ask for. It is not to inform or change the Deity; for there is no variableness, nor shadow of turning with Him. He is of one mind, and no one can turn Him, and "what His soul desires, that He does." It is not inconsistent with the doctrine of divine immutability that one of the unchanging properties of His nature is that He is the hearer of prayer, and that He is not less immutably a prayer-hearing God than He is a God of rectitude and truth. It is true that His counsels never change; but it is equally true that no small part of them were formed in the foreknowledge of all those supplications by which He had previously resolved to be influenced, and which were regarded by Him as the appointed means by which His purposes are carried into effect, and which as truly enter into, and form a part of His purposes as the ends themselves which His purposes secure.

The duty and the privilege of prayer, therefore, are not embarrassed, but sanctioned and encouraged, by the immutability of the divine purposes. There is no mysticism about this plain subject. Prayer itself is just what it purports to be; its object is just what it purports to be, and that is to move the Deity, who from eternity determined to be thus moved, to bestow what the suppliant solicits. The whole field of reason and argument is therefore open to the mind of the petitioner when he goes to the throne of grace; it is his privilege, with heart-felt sincerity, humility, and urgency, to suggest all those considerations which, in the view of a devout mind, may operate as reasons for obtaining his request.

No reasonable man expects to receive a favorable answer to an unreasonable request. We ought not to solicit either of God or man that which is not fitting and proper to be bestowed. Such a request would be an insult to him to whom it is presented; it would be a reproach to him who offers. When a child requests a favor from a parent, or a subject makes a request to his prince, they are interested in making their cause good, and may be expected to set forth the grounds and reasons of their petition. God regards the supplications of men as neither an unnatural nor arbitrary means of procuring the good they crave. He never acts without reason, and has good reasons for requiring them to pray. He is the most reasonable Being in the universe, and therefore the most easily and certainly influenced by considerations which have weight with a wise and benevolent mind; so that when requests are urged at His throne by befitting considerations, they are sure to meet with favor unless there are other and stronger considerations known to Him why it should be denied.

It is true that men sometimes pray without making use of

argument in prayer; when they do so, it is more generally to be attributed to one of two causes: (1) Either they are shut up and have no enlargement of thought, and no such spiritual perceptions and sensibility as enable them to seize upon and amplify the grounds of their requests; or (2) they are too full to utter them, and can only comprehend them in those brief and compendious ejaculations which are expressive of intense desire, and those pithy and importunate entreaties which, while they forbid amplification, are instead of volumes of argument.

In almost every state of mind, they suggest the reasons why they pray and why God should answer. Did they worship an idol god, they might rest satisfied with the unmeaning repetition of their requests, as did the priests of Baal, when "from morning to evening," they cried out, "O Baal, hear us! O Baal, hear us!" This was monotonous, senseless vociferation, and had none of the properties of prayer. The man of God who stood by, and listened to this noisy, tumultuous worship, offered a brief and ardent supplication, every word of which was full of thought. "And it came to pass at the time of the evening sacrifice, that Elijah came near and said, 'Lord God of Abraham, Isaac, and Israel! Let it be known this day that Thou art God in Israel, and that I am Thy servant, and that I have done all these things at Thy word. Hear me, O Lord hear me, that this people may know that Thou art the Lord God, and that Thou hast turned their hearts back again' " (1 Kings 18:36–37). The argument is perfect. If God would be known as God in Israel; if He would be honored for the faithfulness of His promises to Abraham and his seed; if He would publicly confirm the mission of His own prophet, and reclaim His backsliding people; the appeal is one which could not be resisted.

The power of prayer consists not in vapid and vain repetitions, but in affecting thoughts, presented in all the fervency of desire, and all the simplicity and humility of faith. Such was the prayer of Abraham when he interceded for Sodom; such was the prayer of Jacob when, "as a prince he had power with God and with man, and prevailed"; such was the prayer of Moses when he entreated that the divine anger might be turned away from the congregation of Israel; such was the prayer of Hezekiah when he received the menacing message of the proud king of Assyria; such was the prayer of Nehemiah and Daniel when they interceded for the restoration of the exiled Jews; and such was that wonderful prayer of the Savior with and for His disciples, uttered just before His crucifixion.

If the reader will turn to these supplications and analyze them, he will be surprised to find how replete they are with thought and argument. They are remarkable for their energy as well as for their simplicity; nor is it possible for a devout mind to repeat these impressive and earnest pleadings with God without feeling their force, and perceiving that reason and argument are not out of place in prayer. "Oh, that I knew where I might find Him! I would come near even to His seat. I would order my speech before Him, and fill my mouth with arguments" (Job 23:3–4)! Here lies the power of prayer. It is to plead with God as a man expostulates with his friend. Who will question that prayer has power with God, when he hears the voice to Moses as he was about to intercede for idolatrous Israel: "Let Me alone, that My wrath may wax hot against them" (Exodus 32:10)! And how has it power? Not by any mechanical force or physical impulse, but by its moral energy; by its spirit, by its reasons and arguments, by the force of all those considerations by which a benevolent mind is moved to express its bounty, a gracious mind the tenderness and riches of its compassions, and the immutable mind to evince itself the prayer-hearing and prayer-answering God.

The strong arguments, the prevalent reasons in prayer, are drawn from God Himself. "For Thine is the kingdom, the power, and the glory." This shuts out all arguments drawn from the creature, from any merit we have as well as any in those around us. The best of men have no worthiness to plead. "We do not," says the captive suppliant in Babylon, "present our supplications before thee for our righteousnesses." They are rebel men who pray. They may plead their own misery, their wants, their wretchedness, and their vileness; but the fullness on which they rely is His fullness; the merit they plead is His merit; the bounty and grace they ask are His bounty and grace; and the glory of giving is His, and will redound to Him forever. All the divine perfections harmonize in bestowing blessings on the guilty and ill deserving. "Mercy and truth have met together; righteousness and peace have kissed each other" (Psalm 85:10). The medium of communication between heaven and earth is one. "Let no man," said the apostle, "glory in men. For all things are yours; whether Paul or Apollos, or the world, or life or death, or things present or things to come; all are yours, and ye are Christ's, and Christ is God's" (1 Corinthians 3:21–23).

The man who orders his cause wisely most honors the God of heaven. He makes his appeal to the divine nature, to the divine providence, to the redemption by His Son. His arguments are drawn from the knowledge and love of God, and from the revealed principles of His government and grace. The divine kingdom and glory furnish him with arguments. His reliance on the promises furnishes him with arguments. When tempted not to pray because he himself is so vile; when his heart is shut up, and his lips are well nigh sealed in silence by the humbling sense of his own ill-desert and shame; when most depressed and most discouraged, and almost crushed to hopeless despondence because he can find nothing in his past history or his present character that can give him courage and hope, then it is that the boundless all-sufficiency and illimitable grace of the great Hearer of prayer inspirits his otherwise discouraged heart, and his language is, "Give, O Lord; for Thine it is to give. I have nothing, but all is Thine. I am nothing, but Thou art all in all. I am poor, miserable, and vile; but Thine is the kingdom, and the power, and the glory. All is Thine; Thou hast all authority. All that is beautiful and great is Thine, and from Thee."

No matter how great the boon we seek, or how undeserved or how far above our reach; no matter how urgent the necessity, or how wonderful the relief we pray and hope for, if there are reasons for giving it to be found in the wisdom, goodness, power, mercy, rectitude, and glory of the great God, or in any of the forms of His boundless sufficiency, or in any of the manifestations of His great and glorious name; and if they can be perceived and felt and presented at the mercy seat, of this one thing we may be assured, the suppliant shall not be sent away empty.

When Abraham interceded for Sodom, his argument rested on the moral rectitude of God. This was the only consideration he urged, and it prevailed. God could not destroy the righteous with the wicked.

The prayer of Jacob, on his return to the land of his fathers, when met by his enraged brother Esau, rested on the divine faithfulness. God had said, "Return to thy country, and to thy kindred, and I will deal well with thee." The best he could say to God in prayer was what God had promised him. He turned the promises of God into petitions, and was emboldened to say, "I will not let Thee go until Thou bless me."

The intercession of Moses for the idolatrous Israelites was founded on the divine honor and glory. "If Thou smite this people, then the Egyptians shall hear of it, and tell it to the inhabitants of this land." Such, too, was the argument of Joshua when he rent his clothes, and fell to the earth upon his face before the ark, and said, "Alas, O Lord God! What shall I say when Israel turneth their back before their enemies? For the Canaanites, and the inhabitants of the land, shall hear of it; and what wilt Thou do unto Thy great name" (Joshua 7: 8–9)?

That memorable prayer of Jehoshaphat, when the Israelites were invaded by the allied powers of Moab, Ammon, and Edom, rested its expostulations upon God's supremacy and power, His grant of the Holy Land to Israel, His promise to deliver them out of the hand of their enemies, and upon the patient hope and expectation of His people upon Him alone.

These are but specimens of the supplications recorded throughout the entire Scriptures, all of which partake of the same high and disinterested character. One cannot read them without seeing that the urgency and energy of every request rests upon some appeal to the glory of the divine name. Not only are they replete with reason and argument, but with considerations drawn from this high source. They do not consist of rhetorical flourishes, but of weighty and solemn thoughts, uttered in the simplicity, tenderness, and solemnity of true devotion; and while they are expressive of the spirit of adoption, are also expressive of sacred awe of the divine majesty; while they disclaim reliance on other helpers, take hold of God's strength because it is the object and the encouragement of prayer to honor Him. It is not the strength of the creature that gives prayer its energy, but his weakness; nor is it the creature's authority, but God's; nor is it the work or the worthiness of man on which it rests, but the work of God; nor is it man's glory that it seeks, but God's; nor are any of its resources found in man, but in God alone.

It is delightful also to observe the strong confidence of prayer when it rests its pleadings on such arguments as these. While it becomes us to call upon God with a humble and submissive mind, it is no less our duty and privilege to call upon Him with a confiding one. Requests as large and comprehensive as those expressed in the Lord's Prayer demand strong confidence in God. We approach His throne as creatures and as sinners, in all dependence and poverty, in all emptiness and ignorance, in all weakness and pollution, for blessings which we ourselves can neither deserve nor procure, and which no created being can deserve or procure for us.

To approach with holy and joyful confidence we must acquaint ourselves with God; we must ascertain the foundations for confidence that are realized in His all-sufficiency and fullness; and while we turn away with suspicion and distrust from all others, look beyond them all to Him with that affectionate and confiding spirit that is warranted by His infinite and unchanging perfections, and the sacrifice which has opened a new and living way to His throne. "They that trust in the Lord shall be as Mount Zion, which cannot be moved, but abideth forever" (Psalm 125:1). "Though He slay me, yet will I trust in Him" (Job 13:15). "How great is Thy goodness towards them that fear Thee, to them that trust in Thee before the sons of men" (Psalm 31:19)! "Hath He said it, and shall He not do it" (Numbers 23:19)? Such is prayer's confidence.

The people of God have sometimes strong confidence and great boldness in this exercise, because great grace is upon them. There are three things which invigorate and inspirit this confidence: "For thine is the *kingdom*, the *power*, and the *glory*."

"Thine is the *kingdom*." What we solicit belongs to God, and He has it to give. We cannot ask too much, we cannot hope too much from Him, because universal sovereignty belongs to Him; the essential kingdom of the universe, extending itself over the worlds of matter and of mind, of nature and of grace, is His unborrowed, underived, eternal prerogative. He is "God over all, blessed forever." He stands supreme among the whole intelligent creation; the ascendancy of His nature and the infinite superiority of all that belongs to it give Him a right to all things, make Him their owner and proprietor, and invest Him with the natural and moral right, the sovereign and uncontrollable right of giving. This is a reason for both our asking and His giving.

If men claim the right of disposing of what belongs to them, much more has He the right to do what He will with His own. He has it to bestow in plenteousness which no thought can limit. Giving does not impoverish Him, neither does withholding enrich Him. He can satisfy the most ample wishes. His encouraging language is, "Ask and it shall be given you. Let all your wants be upon Me, for I am God, all-sufficient." The greater and more valuable the blessings we desire, the more confident may we be of receiving them in answer to prayer. It is related of Alexander the Great that on one occasion he told the philosopher Anaxarchus to go to his treasurer and ask what he wanted. The treasurer was surprised at the greatness of the sum, and refused to pay it without consulting his prince. "It seemed," said he, "too much for one man to receive." The reply of his sovereign was, "It is not too much for Alexander to give. He does honor to my riches and liberality by so large a request." The Scripture says, "Thine is the kingdom!" The princely liberality of the King of the universe can no more be exhausted than His inexhaustible fullness and all-sufficiency. He is not more a boundless ocean of blessedness than of munificence. He is the great Benefactor as truly as the great King. He takes a God-like pleasure in answering the supplications of His people. His kingdom itself is extended and promoted by it; the greater the blessing, the more does His benevolent and liberal heart express itself, and the more is it gratified and honored by the gift.

"Thine is the *power*." His too is the power as well as the kingdom. That which He is pleased to will, He is able to bestow. If His power to bestow were more limited than His right or His disposition to give, there would be no strong foundation for confidence in prayer. If there were a single blessing He could not give, our confidence in Him would be shaken for every blessing. Should His power fail in one instance, it would be impossible for us to know that it would not fail in ten thousand instances, and in those in which the spirit of prayer feels the deepest interest.

The confidence of the father of the faithful was encouraged by the declaration, "I am the Almighty God." Job was comforted with the thought, "I know that Thou canst do every thing." And the devout Psalmist gloried in the truth, "Our God is in the heavens; He hath done whatever He hath pleased."

The omnipotence of God has more than a little to do with the spirit of prayer. Strong is His hand, and high is His right hand. He has a God-like arm as well as a God-like heart. Be the good we crave what it may, spiritual or temporal, relating to ourselves or others, be it ever so retired and hidden from the eye or beyond the reach of creatures, He can bestow it with infinite ease. He speaks and it is done. He commands and it stands fast. Nothing can hinder, nothing can disappoint, and nothing can weary Him. "Whatsoever His soul desireth, that He doeth" (Job 23:13). Difficulties, enemies, unworthiness, ill desert, and the constant recurrence of our wants, form no obstacle to His bounty. If the good we crave is found anywhere in the wide universe, He can lay it at our feet; or if it is not in being, His all-powerful word can create it, and give existence to what had no existence before.

He can do all things. What an argument for prayer, to say, "Thine is the power!" And the result is:

"Thine is the *glory*!" Here the argument and the ground of confidence become firm and invincible. His is the glory of being the Hearer of prayer; for this is His name, and this is His memorial to all generations. His is the glory of this wondrous condescension and grace; for He stoops to man who is a worm, and to sinful man who has provoked His wrath. His is the glory of giving, of giving where there is no merit and no recompense; of giving so variously and so largely. His goodness, wisdom, power, justice, faithfulness, mercy, and sovereignty all appear in their loveliness, beauty, and divine splendor in answering prayer. He gives what spotless innocence cannot claim, what a world could not buy; and, by so doing, His glory is both secured and advanced.

It is great glory which He spreads over the works of His hands; but in giving what His people pray for there is glory beyond all the glories of the natural world. Such a mind as [Isaac] Newton's, looking out on the fields of space, sprinkled with suns for other systems as a meadow is decked with flowers, beholds in these wondrous works a glory which intelligence and piety delight to contemplate. But the glory of God as the Hearer of prayer, as the greatest of all givers, as the Author and Sustainer of the new creation in the hearts of men and in this apostate world, with all its holiness, all its hopes, all its joys, surpasses it all, shines when the sun has gone out, and the cycles of time have come to a close.

"Thine is the kingdom, and the power, and the glory, *forever*!" The spirit of prayer is a far-reaching spirit; it looks into eternity. The kingdom, and the power, and the glory are Thine always; forever shall they shine in growing and augmented splendor. Hereafter and throughout ceaseless ages, "as it was in the beginning, is now, and ever shall be, world without end," the God of heaven is exalted as the Hearer of prayer.

The three great arguments in prayer are therefore the three

strong grounds of the suppliant's confidence. The God we worship commands that confidence for what He is, sustains it by what He has said and done, perpetuates it by what He is still able and willing to do, and will have the glory of doing in answer to the supplications of His people.

Nor is it any reason why that confidence should be shaken that sometimes He defers our requests or withholds the solicited blessing. If we ask for what is best, we know that He hears us; while, if through ignorance, infirmity, or sin we fail in doing this, we still know that He will not be unmindful of our highest good, though He exercises His own wisdom and discretion in declining as well as granting our requests. There is no ground for discouragement in prayer where the Christian casts all His care on God; nor, on the other hand, is there any motive to prayer, or any comfort in this delightful duty, where these divine resources are lost sight of. We become wise in His wisdom, mighty in His power, and comforted in His all-sufficiency when His wisdom guides us, when we take hold of His everlasting strength, and when, worms as we are, His all-sufficiency influences our prayers and actuates our conduct.

There is no place for discouragement, no room for despondency, so long as the kingdom, the power, and the glory are the Lord's. Thinking of ourselves only, and of our sins, wants, and dangers, we have good cause for apprehension. But there is One who is God over all, who has all hearts in His hands and all events under His control, whom heaven and earth and sea obey, who is able to save and to destroy, before whom angels bow and devils tremble, and though we are perfect weakness, yet is His grace sufficient, and His glory our reward.

Prayer terminates in praise. The Father of mercies and the God of all grace is worthy to be exalted. Those excellencies of the divine nature we most dwell upon in prayer, and those considerations we make use of as our strongest arguments at the throne of grace, the more we contemplate them, become expressive of reverence and honor, kindle into gratitude and joy, and are the themes of admiring song. While we take encouragement in our prayers because the kingdom, power, and glory are the Lord's, we necessarily desire that He may be exalted and glorified, and that we may ascribe to Him the glory due to His holy name.

On that great occasion when the princes and people of Israel offered so willingly for building the temple, "David blessed the Lord, before all the congregation. And David said, 'Blessed be Thou, Lord God of Israel, our Father, forever and ever. Thine, O Lord, is the greatness, and the power, and the glory, and the victory, and the majesty; for all that is in the heaven and in the earth is Thine; Thine is the kingdom, O Lord, and Thou art exalted as head above all. Both riches and honor come of Thee, and Thou reignest over all; and in Thine hand is power and might, and Thine it is to make great, and to give strength unto all. Now, therefore, O God, we thank Thee, and praise Thy glorious name' " (1 Chronicles 29:10–13). Paul's ascription was, "Now unto the King eternal, immortal, invisible, the only wise God, be honor and glory, forever and ever" (1 Timothy 1:17). "Whoso offereth praise," said God, "glorifieth Me" (Psalm 50:23). Praise engages Him to hear.

Sing praises unto God, ye kingdoms of the earth. Oh, sing praises unto the Lord! Talk of Him, speak forth His name; say of Him, "Thine is the kingdom! The unbounded, universal kingdom of nature, providence, and grace, is Thine! The visible and the invisible, the kingdom above and the kingdom below, the kingdom of grace and the kingdom of justice, are Thine. Thy kingdom is an everlasting kingdom, and of Thy dominion there is no end. Above the heavens, beyond the earth, below the ocean, Thy kingdom is prepared, O God, and

Thou reignest forever. The kingdoms of this world are but little spots of earth compared with Thy vast dominions, O Thou sovereign Lord; and the princes of this world are but vanity compared with Thee. Thine, too, is the power. Who, O Lord, is a strong Lord like unto Thee, or to Thy faithfulness round about Thee! What wonders hast Thou done, O Thou who art very great, and art clothed with majesty! Thou layest the beams of Thy chambers in the mighty waters; Thou makest the clouds Thy chariot, and walkest upon the wings of the wind. The Lord God omnipotent reigneth, and let the earth rejoice! The glory is Thine. The glory of creatures is fallen, and their memory forgotten. The flower of Lebanon, and the beauty of Bashan and Carmel languish; but Thy glory is above the earth and the heavens. Glorious art Thou in holiness, fearful in praises, doing wonders."

As a great God and a great King, decked as He is with light as with a garment, and arrayed in majesty and excellency, we may hope in Him, and we may praise Him. The kingdom, the power, and the glory are His forever. The Lord shall reign forever and ever. What a word is that one word "forever!" Nothing can increase, nothing diminish, nothing terminate the kingdom, power, and glory of God. Always glorious, always reigning in the fullness of His glory, He is God over all, blessed for evermore.

And to these ascriptions, the spirit of prayer adds its hearty and emphatic "Amen!" This is a term of great emphasis. The original word signifies solidity, not to be shaken; truth that stands firm. "He which testifieth these things saith, 'I come quickly; amen.' *Even so,* come, Lord Jesus" (Revelation 22:20). We utter this emphatic term in testimony of our desire to be heard, and of our assurance of being so. "Lord, Thou hast heard the desire of the humble; Thou wilt prepare their heart, for Thou wilt cause Thine ear to hear." The desire and prayer for blessings always has some measure of assurance of them in God's own time and way. Let the kingdom be the Lord's; let the power and the glory be His forever. Let Him be exalted, and all creatures lie low at His footstool!

Prayer and praise may not be given to earth and creatures. We pay no such homage to the painting of the artist, the statue of the sculptor, nor to any image graven by art of man's device, nor to hero gods nor martyred saints. To God alone give glory. "Blessed be the Lord God, the God of Israel, who only doeth wondrous things! And blessed be His glorious name forever! And let the whole earth be filled with His glory, amen and amen" (Psalm 72:18–19).

Thus it is that in our prayers we praise Him. The spirit of the closet and the sanctuary are closely allied to the spirit of heaven. At His throne of grace, we are but a little distance from His throne of glory. The nearer we come to God, the more evidence have we that we shall dwell with God. He who would be fitted for heaven must be much in prayer while on the earth.

Alas, how little account do even God's own people make of prayer! The pulse of spiritual life would never become low in the bosom of Christians if they knew more of the power of prayer. The dews of mercy would not be so often and so long restrained, nor the rain of heaven withheld, nor its clouds shut up, if they knew what may be so easily known of the power and preciousness of prayer. God would remember His covenant, His Church would flourish like the cedar in Lebanon and grow as the vine, were she more faithful and diligent in thus proving the faithfulness and love of her divine Lord. "Come, thou north wind, and blow thou south, and breathe upon thy garden, that the spices thereof may flow forth" (Song of Solomon 4:16).

How marvelous, too, is it that wicked men never pray, or

pray so little! What a wonderful foundation is laid for prayer in the nature of the Deity, and at the mercy seat where the blood of Jesus pleads for the chief of sinners! Oh, that the thoughtless, impenitent reader of these humble pages might be allured by them to the throne of the heavenly grace! He must live a life of prayer who would die a death of praise.

To those who love to pray, this author takes leave to address this last paragraph. Let the Christian reader call to mind what and where he would have been without prayer; let him value the privilege more than the gold of Ophir. If in his more favored seasons of fellowship with his heavenly Father he seems sometimes to leave these earthly regions behind him, and take his flight almost within the veil, let him thank God and take courage. The earthly house of his tabernacle will soon be dissolved, and those who here truly call God their Father will bow with the great multitude which no man can number, and ascribe blessing and honor, glory and thanksgiving, and power and might, to Him who is seated on the throne and to the Lamb. Nothing is more certain than that the affectionate appeal, "Our Father, who art in heaven," will terminate in the holy ardor of the everlasting song. Wondrous wisdom, wondrous goodness, and wondrous grace are the themes of their song. Wonders still greater must remain untold and uncelebrated. The piety of heaven is progressive, though sinless; their love is a constant, bright, and glowing flame; their joy is unspeakable and full of glory. The thoughts they utter and the emotions which swell their song are the most delightful, the most tender, the most pure, elevated, and rapturous. Creatures are forgotten there, and God alone is exalted. Created grandeur fades; the glory of all creatures vanishes. What a joyous, what a ravishing song, when ten thousand times ten thousand, and thousands of thousands, "as the voice of many waters, and as the voice of mighty thunderings, and as the voice of harpers harping with their harps," unite in the ascription, "Unto Him that loved us, and washed us from our sins in His own blood, and hath made us kings and priests unto God, even His Father; to Him be glory and dominion, forever and ever!"

The more the reader is imbued with the spirit of heaven, and the nearer he draws to that unseen world, the less will he think, feel, and speak of meaner things and meaner joys, and the more will his heart and tongue be filled with praise. Oh, that men would praise the Lord for His goodness, for His wonderful works to the children of men! "To Thee all angels cry aloud; the heavens and all the powers that are therein. To Thee, Cherubim and Seraphim continually do cry, 'Holy, holy, holy, Lord God of Sabaoth; heaven and earth are full of the majesty of Thy glory! The glorious company of the apostles praise Thee, the goodly fellowship of the prophets praise Thee, the noble army of martyrs praise Thee. The holy Church throughout all the world doth praise Thee. Let every thing that hath breath praise the Lord!' "

Praise is the appropriate employment of the heavenly world. Or, rather, it is the employment which is there interwoven with all other employments. The day is not far distant when those who truly offer this prayer will have less to ask for than to enjoy; nothing daily to confess, because they will sin no more; no wants, no trials to spread before the throne of infinite mercy, because every want shall be supplied, and all tears shall be wiped from every eye. His name shall then be every where hallowed; His kingdom shall have come in its glory. They themselves, clothed in white robes, and with palms in their hands, shall bow before the throne of God, and serve Him day and night in His temple. They shall hear the voice of much people in heaven, and with them shall cry "Hallelujah, glory, salvation, honor and power to the Lord our God!" And again they shall say, "HALLELUJAH!"